BRANCH LINES AROUND CHARD AND YEOVIL
from Taunton, Durston and Castle Cary

Vic Mitchell and Keith Smith

MP Middleton Press

Cover picture: Ex-GWR 0-4-2T no. 1451 stands alongside ex-SR coaches at Yeovil Town on 26th October 1963. The two companies had operated the station jointly for many years, but the area is now a bland car park. (E.Wilmshurst)

Published March 1999

ISBN 1 901706 30 3

© Middleton Press, 1999

Design Deborah Esher

Published by
 Middleton Press
 Easebourne Lane
 Midhurst, West Sussex
 GU29 9AZ
Tel: 01730 813169
Fax: 01730 812601

Printed & bound by Biddles Ltd,
 Guildford and Kings Lynn

CONTENTS

1.	Taunton to Chard Junction	1- 26
2.	Durston to Yeovil Town	27- 80
3.	Castle Cary to Yeovil Junction	81-112
4.	Around Yeovil	113-120

INDEX

30	Athelney	29	Lyng Halt
81	Castle Cary	92	Marston Magna
14	Chard Central	41	Martock
24	Chard Junction	46	Montacute
21	Chard Town Goods	1	Taunton
13	Donyatt Halt	39	Thorney and Kingsbury Halt
27	Durston	3	Thornfalcon
6	Hatch	87	Sparkford
49	Hendford	104	Yeovil Junction
10	Ilminster	94	Yeovil Pen Mill
9	Ilton Halt	57	Yeovil Town
34	Langport West		

ACKNOWLEDGEMENTS

In addition to those mentioned in the photographic credits, we would like to thank the following for assistance received: W.R.Burton, R.M.Casserley, G.Croughton, M.Dart, M.King, N.Langridge, D.R.Phillips, Mr D. & Dr S.Salter, J.J.Smith, E.Youldon and, as always, our wives for all their help and encouragement.

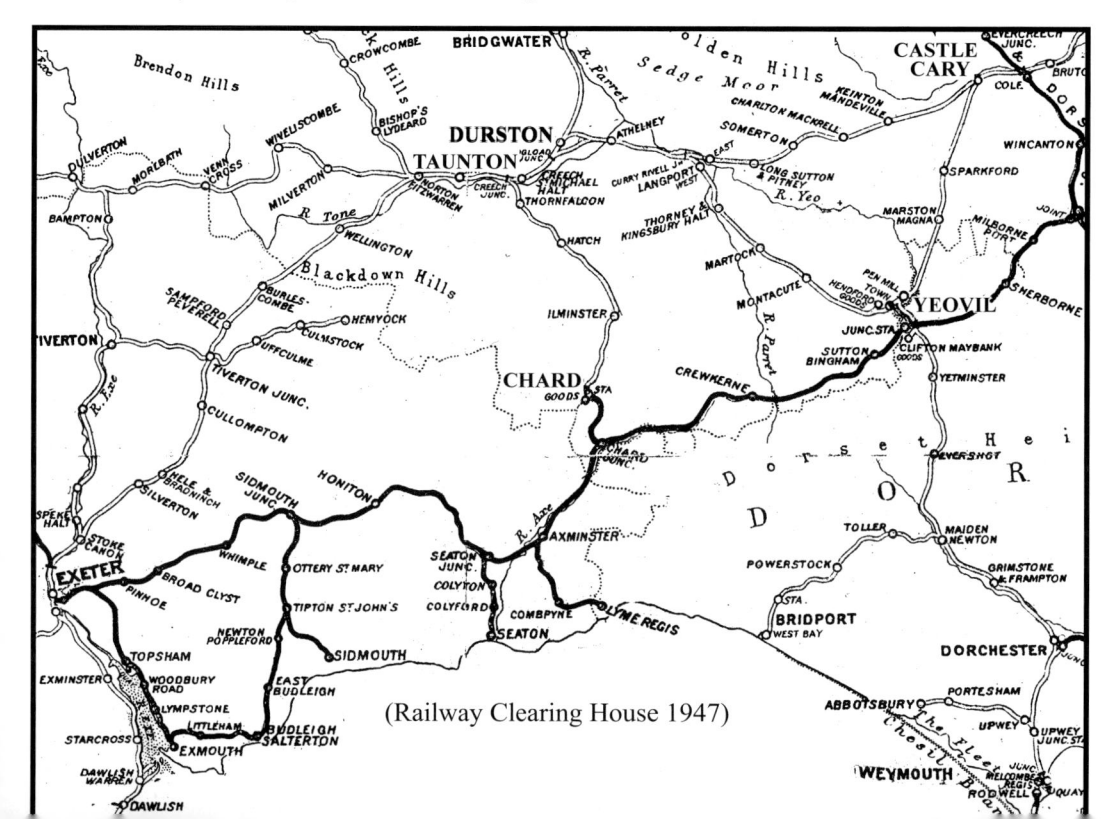

(Railway Clearing House 1947)

GEOGRAPHICAL SETTING

The historic market town of Chard stands on Upper Greensand, near the watershed of the Rivers Axe and Isle. The railway ran in the shallow valley of the latter as far as Ilminster, mainly on Lower Lias Clay. North thereof, it traversed higher undulating ground, finally descending into the Tone Valley and turning west to Taunton.

The old established market town of Yeovil is situated on the ridge of Yeovil Sands, west of the point at which it is bisected by the north flowing River Yeo. The gap created was used by the builders of the line from Castle Cary, south to Weymouth.

Castle Cary is located on high ground south of the junction, the main line being in the valley of the River Brue. The Weymouth branch takes an undulating course to Yeovil, crossing over a number of watercourses, notably the River Cam, south of Sparkford. Much of the route is on clay and passes through agricultural land in its entirety.

The same remarks apply to the route north to Durston betwen Yeovil and Martock. However, north thereof the route descends onto the Alluvium of the moors surrounding the Rivers Parrett and Tone for the remainder of the journey to Durston. There are two brief excursions onto higher ground, in the vicinity of Langport and Athelney.

Most of the southern portion of the route has disappeared under the A3088. The maps are at the scale of 25ins to 1 mile, unless otherwise stated; north is at the top in all cases.

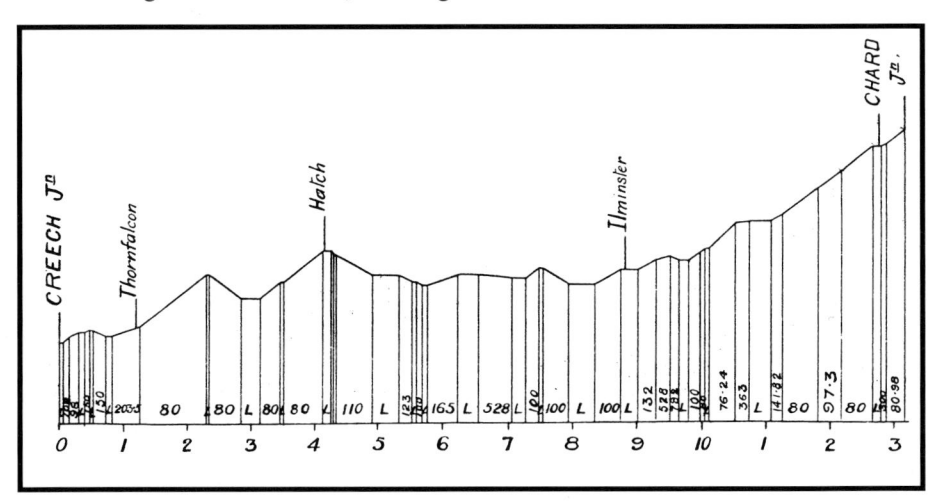

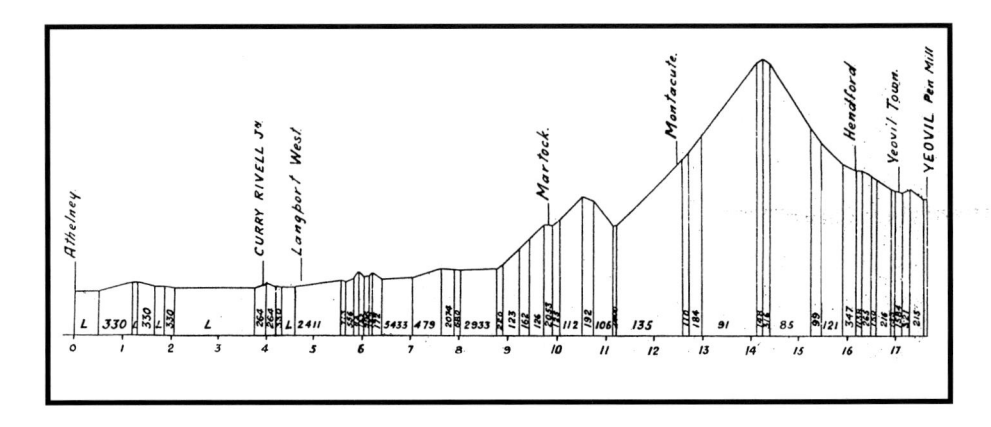

HISTORICAL BACKGROUND

The Bristol & Exeter Railway was opened south to Taunton on 1st July 1842 and the 1845 Wilts, Somerset & Weymouth Railway Company's line from Frome came into use as far as Yeovil on 1st September 1856; completion to Weymouth was four months later. Both these routes were built to the broad gauge of 7ft 0¼ins and the companies became part of the Great Western Railway in 1876 and 1850 respectively.

The BER was authorised to construct a branch from Durston to Yeovil in 1845, but it did not open until 1st October 1853 (freight from 26th) and then only as far as Hendford, on the outskirts of Yeovil. It was extended to link with the Weymouth route at Yeovil Pen Mill on 2nd February 1857.

The London & South Western Railway reached Yeovil (Hendford) from Sherborne on 1st June 1860 (freight from 1st September). Yeovil Junction and the route to Exeter came into use on 19th July of that year. Hendford closed to passengers and was replaced by Yeovil Town on 1st June 1861 and a line to connect it with Yeovil Junction was opened on the same day. Direct running from Sherborne to Yeovil Town ceased on 1st January 1870. A freight transfer line from the Weymouth route to Yeovil Junction (Clifton Maybank) was in use from June 1864 until 7th June 1937.

Chard received its first train on 8th May 1863, when a branch was opened from the 1860 LSWR main line and operated by that company from the outset. The Chard & Taunton Railway obtained an Act in 1861, the powers of which were acquired by the BER. Their broad gauge line was opened to passengers on 11th September 1866, goods services starting in the following March. A new station was provided and was known as Chard Joint (Central from 1949). The LSWR terminus became Chard Town and remained in passenger use until 30th December 1916. Thereafter the entire route to Chard Junction was operated by the GWR.

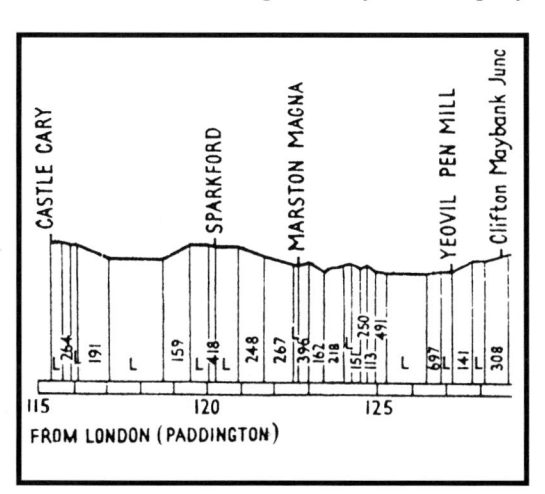

Broad gauge was abandoned on the Durston-Yeovil line in June 1879, although it had been dual gauge since November 1867. The Castle Cary-Yeovil section was narrowed in June 1874 and was double track from 1881 until 12th May 1968. The Taunton-Chard branch remained broad gauge as long as possible, in order to reduce the risk of LSWR trains reaching Taunton; conversion took place in July 1891.

As part of a scheme to reduce journey times between London and the West of England, the GWR built a direct link between Castle Cary and Taunton in 1905-06, this bypassing Durston.

The LSWR lines became part of the Southern Railway in 1923 and the Southern Region of British Railways upon nationalisation in 1948. The GWR lines formed the Western Region and all ex-SR routes in the area were incorporated therein in January 1963. An anomaly was the transfer of the Creech Junction-Chard Junction section to the Southern Region in 1950, although operated by the Western Region. The line was closed from 3rd February to 7th May 1951 due to a fuel shortage. The Langport West to Yeovil and the Castle Cary to Yeovil sections also went to the Southern Region in 1950.

The Chard route closed to passengers on 10th September 1962, but freight service continued at most stations until 6th July 1964. Closure of the Durston-Yeovil line to passengers took place on 15th June 1964, goods traffic ceasing on 6th July 1964. Closures within the Yeovil area and north thereof are detailed in the captions.

PASSENGER SERVICES

In these notes we consider down trains running at least five days per week over the full length of the line.

Taunton-Chard

The LSWR gradually increased its Chard Junction-Chard Town service from five per day in 1869 to seven in 1890 and twelve in 1914, weekdays only.

The GWR trains between Taunton and Chard in the same years were five, five and seven, but there were also two or three Sunday journeys in the early 1860s only. From 1917, the GWR provided seven trains over the entire route, two extra between the joint and junction stations at Chard and one on Sundays north of Chard.

For most of the life of the line, there were five journeys, weekdays only, with one or two extra south of Chard. This section had a few Southern operated trips on Summer Sundays in 1938-39 to connect with trains to holiday resorts.

Chard Central remained a "frontier" station to the end, with most trains waiting there for long periods.

Taunton -Yeovil

The first timetable showed five weekday and two Sunday trains, but the latter were soon discontinued.

All services commenced at Durston in the early years. There were six or seven trains, weekdays only, for most of the life of the line, with one or two more in the 1930s, most running through to Pen Mill.

Castle Cary - Yeovil

For over a century, the basic service was provided by Westbury-Weymouth stopping trains, with one or two fast trains from Bristol and London each day, the latter ceasing in 1960.

The table indicates the number of down trains between the towns, in selected years.

	Limited stop		Stopping	
	Weekdays	Sundays	Weekdays	Sundays
1890	2	0	4	2
1925	2	0	5	2
1938	3	1	4	2
1951	4	3	7	2
1964	4	0	8	4
1974	7	6	-	-
1989	9	7	-	-
1998	8	3	-	-

November 1890

July 1914

CHARD and CHARD JUNCTION.—London and South Western.

Miles	Week Days only.	mrn	mrn	mrn	aft	aft	c	b	aft	aft	aft	aft	aft	aft
	Joint Station, **Chard** dep.		9 43		1230		2 35	2 45	4 15					
¼	Chard (Town)	6 57	9 46	1118	1233	1 55	2 38	2 48	4 21	5 2	5 45	6 38	8 32	9 22
3¼	**Chard Jn. 128, 131** arr.	7 5	9 54	1126	1241	2 3	2 46	2 56	4 29	5 10	5 53	6 46	8 40	9 30

Miles	Week Days only.	mrn	mrn	mrn	aft	aft	c	b	aft	aft	aft	aft	aft	aft
	Chard Junc. dep.	7 45	1028	1147	1 18	2 13	3 0	3 12	4 42	5 27	6 12	7 28	9 0	9 36
3	Chard (Town)	7 57	1036	1155	1 30	2 21	3 8	3 20	4 50	5 35	6 20	7 36	9 8	9 44
3¼	**Chard (Joint) 48** arr.			1158		2 24	3 11	3 23				7 39		9 47

b Commences on the 17th instant. **c** Will not run after the 16th instant.

uly
914

TAUNTON, CHARD CENTRAL and CHARD JUNCTION

WEEK DAYS ONLY

Miles		am	am		am		am		pm	pm S		pm	pm		pm		pm		pm	pm		pm	
	Taunton dep	6 0			8 0							3 12			4 30					6 45			
3½	Thornfalcon				8 6							3 20			4 36					6 52			
6½	Hatch				8 14							3 29			4 44					7 0			
9¾	Ilton Halt				8 22							3 37			4 52					7 8			
11¼	Ilminster	6 40			8 28							3 43			4 58					7 13			
12	Donyatt Halt				8 32							3 49			5 2					7 17			
15¼	**Chard Central** arr	7 0			8 40							3 57			5 10					7 25			
	dep		8 10				9 34		12 2	1 52			4 7				5 30		6 9			8 43	
18½	**Chard Junction** arr		8 18				9 42		1210	2 0			4 15				5 38		6 17			8 51	

Miles		am		am		am		pm		pm		pm S		pm		pm		pm		pm		pm	
	Chard Junction dep	8 28				1056		1245				2 30		5 4		5 50		6 34				9 30	
3¼	**Chard Central** arr	8 37				11 6		1255				2 39		5 13		5 59		6 43				9 39	
	dep			8 45						1 35				5 15						7 40		9 45	
6½	Donyatt Halt			8 51						1 41				5 21						7 46			
7¼	Ilminster			8 55						1 47				5 25						7 51		9 53	
8¾	Ilton Halt			8 58						1 51				5 29						7 55			
12	Hatch			9 5						2 0				5 36						8 2			
15	Thornfalcon			9 12						2 7				5 43						8 9			
18½	**Taunton** arr			9 21						2 15				5 56						3 17		1016	

S Saturdays only

ept
916

TAUNTON, DURSTON and YEOVIL

WEEK DAYS ONLY

Miles		am		am		am	am		pm		pm		pm S	pm		pm		pm	pm	pm		
	Taunton dep	6 45				9 45			1258				2 10			4 25		5 55	8 20			
2¾	Creech St. Michael Halt	6 50																6 2				
5¾	Durston	6 57											2 20			4 34		6 9	8 29			
7½	Lyng Halt	7 2											2 24			4 38		6 13				
8	Athelney	7 5				9 57			1 10				2 28			4 40		6 17	8 34			
13	Langport West	7 18				10 7			1 20				2 42			4 51		6 26	8 43			
15¼	Thorney & Kingsbury Halt	7 23				1012			1 25				2 49			4 57		6 31	8 48			
18	Martock	7 29				1022			1 31				2 58			5 4		6 37	8 54			
20¾	Montacute	7 37				1029			1 37				3 6			5 13		6 44	9 0			
24½	Hendford Halt	7 45				1037			1 45				3 14			5 21		6 52	9 8			
25½	**Yeovil Town** arr	7 48				1040			1 48				3 17			5 24		6 54	9 11			
	Yeovil Town dep	7 50		8 42		1042	1131		1 51		2 39		3 20	4 28		5 33		6 56	9 13	9 50		
26	**Yeovil Pen Mill** arr	7 54		8 46		1045	1133		1 55		2 41		3 24	4 30		5 37		6 59	9 16	9 52		

Miles		am	am		am		am		am		pm S		pm		pm		pm	pm	pm			
	Yeovil Pen Mill dep	7 5	8 50		9 56		1052		1121		1237		2 25		4 0		5 45	7 50	9 58			
	Yeovil Town arr	7 7	8 52		9 58		1054		1123		1239		2 27		4 2		5 47	7 52	10 0			
½	**Yeovil Town** dep	7 10			10 0				1124		1241				4 8		5 50	7 54				
1½	Hendford Halt	7 15			10 3				1127		1244				4 12		5 54	7 58				
5¼	Montacute	7 24			1012				1136		1253				4 21		6 4	8 7				
8	Martock	7 32			1019				1142		1259				4 28		6 10	8 13				
10¾	Thorney & Kingsbury Halt	7 39			1025				1148		1 5				4 34		6 16	8 19				
13	Langport West	7 45			1030				1157		1 11				4 39		6 21	8 25				
18	Athelney	7 54			1039				12 6		1 21				4 48		6 31	8 35				
18½	Lyng Halt	7 57							12 8		1 23				4 50		6 33	8 37				
20½	Durston	8 2							1213		1 28				4 55		6 38	8 42				
23¼	Creech St. Michael Halt	8 8							1219		1 34				5 1		6 44	8 48				
26	**Taunton** arr	8 14			1052				1225		1 40				5 7		6 51	8 55				

S Saturdays only

ept
963

YEOVIL (Town) and YEOVIL (Pen Mill) SUNDAYS

	pm		pm
Yeovil Town dep	4 12		5 40
Yeovil Pen Mill arr	4 14		5 42
	pm		**pm**
Yeovil Pen Mill dep	4 30		5 52
Yeovil Town arr	4 32		5 54

ept
963

1. Taunton to Chard Junction
TAUNTON

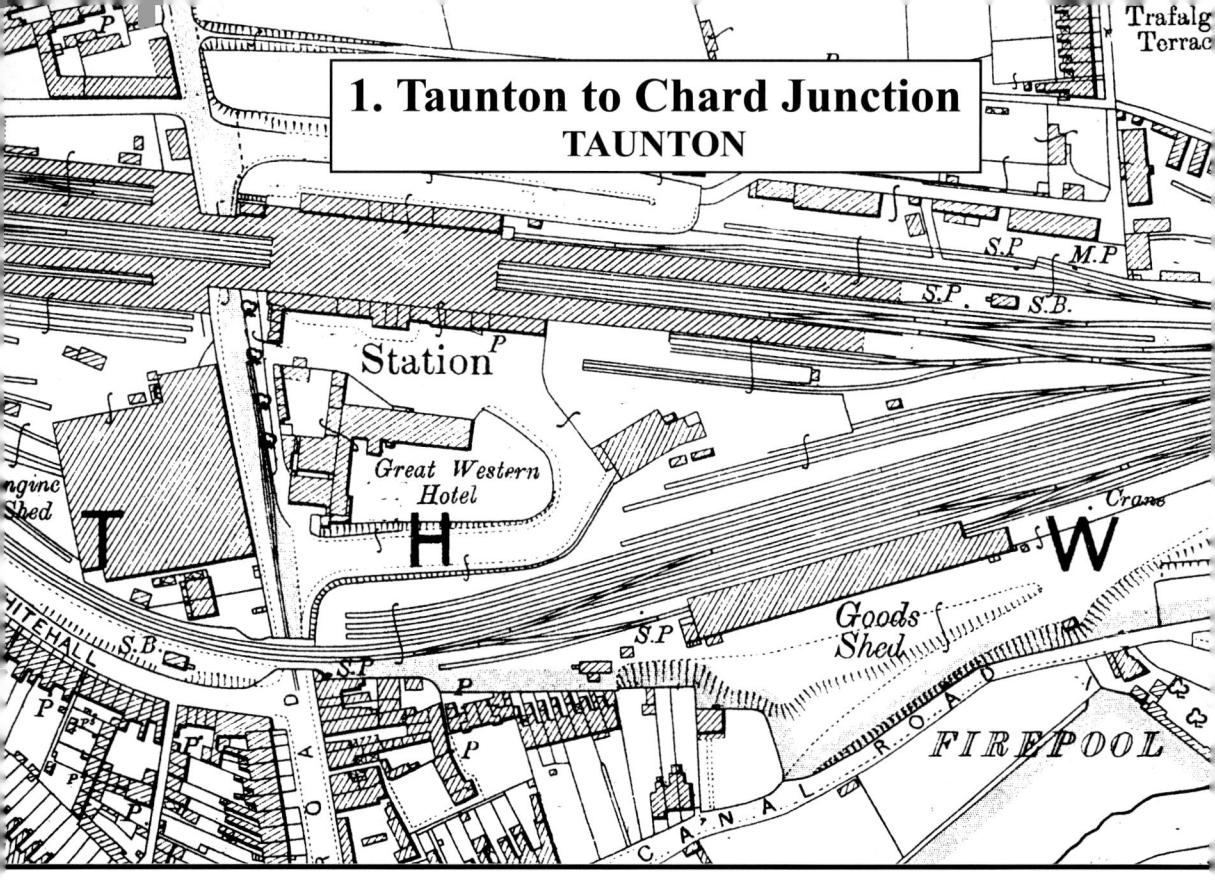

1. A westward view in 1921 shows the overall roof, which was removed prior to the provision of four through platforms in 1931. The two platforms on the left were retained, the bay (numbered 2) usually accommodating the Chard trains. (LGRP/NRM)

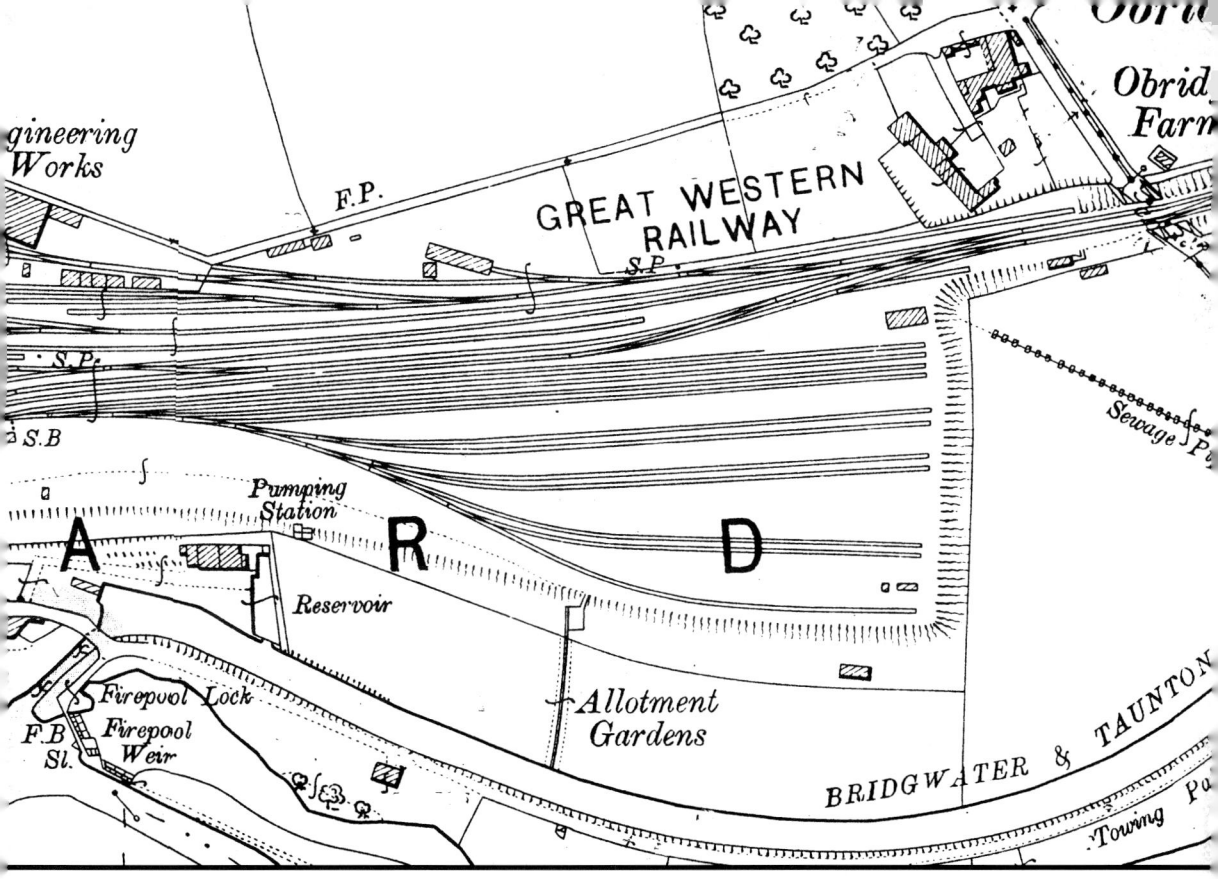

The 1904 survey reveals that there were three through lines. Until 1868, there were two platforms, end to end, on the south side of the lines. Bay platforms were added in 1895. The canal curving across the right page had continued westwards, but in 1896 goods lines were laid in its place. They cross the tramway which is featured in *Exeter and Taunton Tramways* (Middleton Press). The west end of the station is illustrated in our *Branch Line to Minehead*.

2. After the rebuilding, the original platform (left) continued to be numbered 1 and the new island platform became 5 and 6. Four mechanical signal boxes were required, but since 1985 the much simplified layout has been controlled from a panel at the Exeter Signalling Centre. (Lens of Sutton)

THORNFALCON

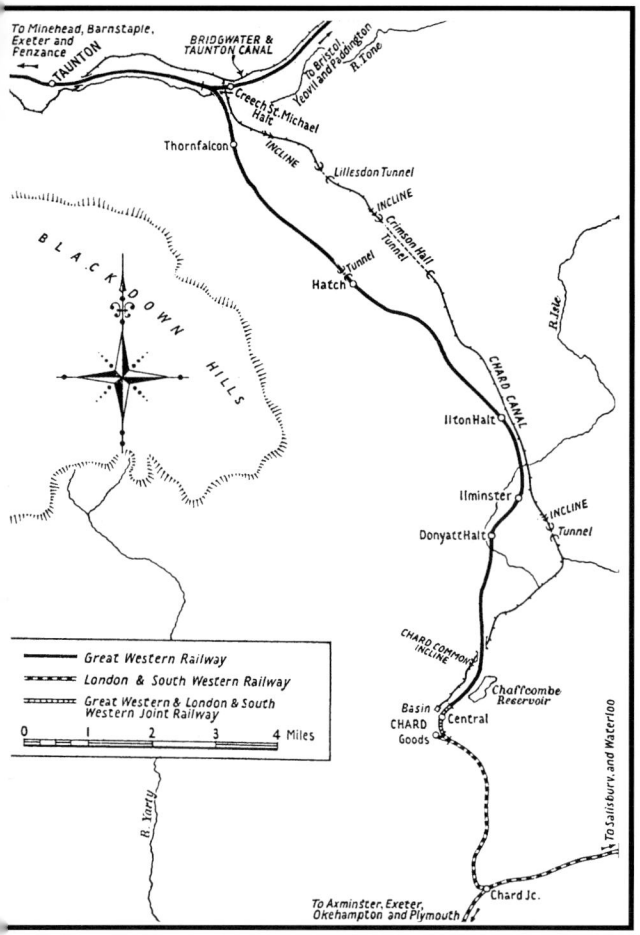

→ The 1946 map at 1 inch to 1 mile shows the commencement of the Chard branch at Creech Junction, the halt for the village being on the main line. There were sidings for the paper mill at the junction from 1875 to 1966.

Thornfalcon	1903	1913	1923	1933
Passenger tickets issued	5053	5581	4140	542
Season tickets issued	*	*	13	-
Parcels forwarded	1507	2207	3013	689
General goods forwarded (tons)	665	802	911	248
Coal and coke received (tons)	546	583	234	83
Other minerals received (tons)	1763	1831	2583	7
General goods received (tons)	1282	1287	701	185
Trucks of livestock handled	-	-	-	-

(*not available)

→ The 1904 survey reveals the unusual and dangerous arrangement of the loop siding which necessitated passengers walking over it. A dual carriageway now traverses this area.

3. Full signalling was provided until October 1912, although the station was never a passing place. It was opened as "Thorne Falcon" in 1871 and renamed "Thorne" in July 1890 and finally became "Thornfalcon" in January 1902. (Lens of Sutton)

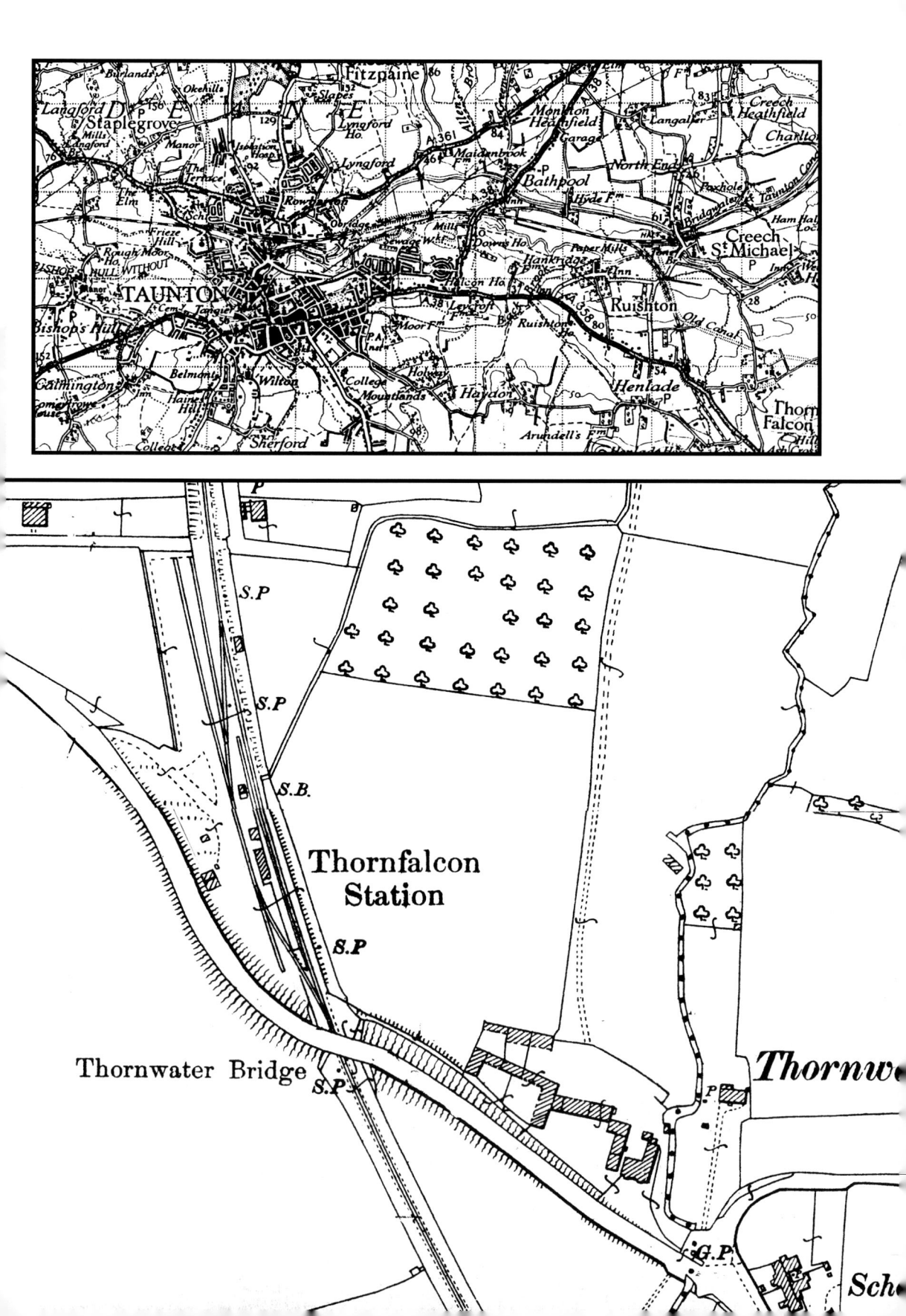

Thornfalcon Station

Thornwater Bridge

Thornw

Sch

4. The 15-lever signal box had been badly sited for vision southwards. A small goods shed can be seen further along the platform. Lamps were provided near the main building only in the final years. (Lens of Sutton)

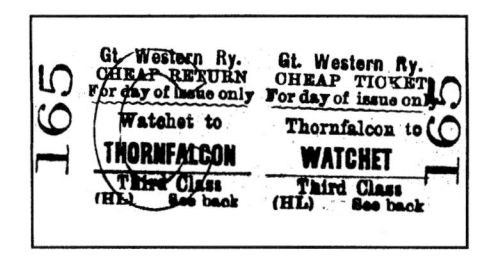

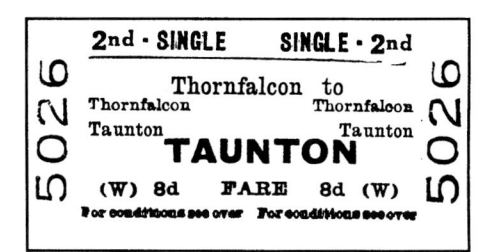

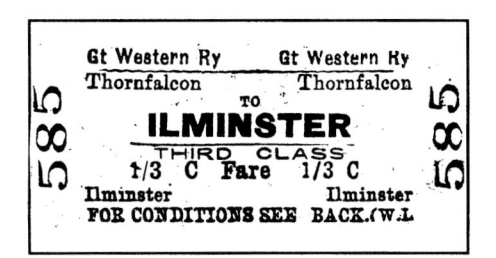

| 2nd · SINGLE   SINGLE · 2nd |
| Thornfalcon to / Thornfalcon to |
| Taunton / Taunton |
| **TAUNTON** |
| (W) 8d   FARE   8d (W) |
| For conditions see over   For conditions see over |
| 5026 | 5026 |

| Gt Western Ry   Gt Western Ry |
| Thornfalcon   Thornfalcon |
| TO |
| **ILMINSTER** |
| THIRD CLASS |
| 1/3 C   Fare   1/3 C |
| Ilminster   Ilminster |
| FOR CONDITIONS SEE BACK.(W.L |
| 585 | 585 |

5.　The "T" sign indicates Termination of a length of temporary speed restriction. The goods yard had a 30cwt. crane (left) and seems busy in this view. It closed on 6th July 1964. (Lens of Sutton)

HATCH

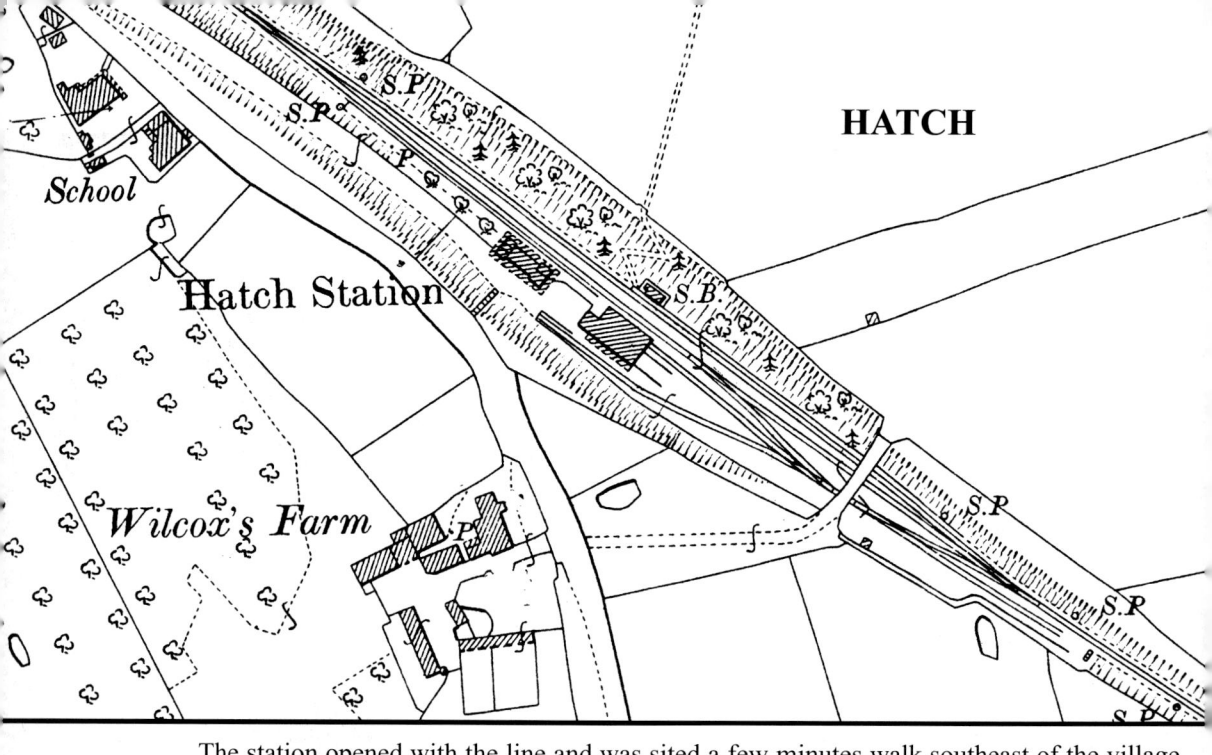

The station opened with the line and was sited a few minutes walk southeast of the village centre. The zig-zag footpath behind the signal box on this 1904 survey gave direct access to Hatch Court. The approach road descends from the top left.

6. A northward view towards the 154yd-long Hatch Tunnel features the classical Brunel-style building found so widely on the GWR. The track comprises bridge rail set on longitudinal timbers, a design used by Brunel for broad gauge track. (Lens of Sutton)

7. The panorama from the occupation bridge includes a crossing and stairway for the footpath and a cattle dock. Legacies from the broad gauge era are the offset siding in the goods shed doorway and the baulk road in the goods loop. The signal box was built in 1892 with 29 levers.
(Lens of Sutton)

Hatch	1903	1913	1923	1933
Passenger tickets issued	9883	10115	10340	3952
Season tickets issued	*	*	28	16
Parcels forwarded	3584	7268	8307	3273
General goods forwarded (tons)	1337	1562	1319	481
Coal and coke received (tons)	941	151	301	86
Other minerals received (tons)	1211	1494	2828	1034
General goods received (tons)	1379	1880	2094	1486
Trucks of livestock handled	83	89	63	29

(* not available)

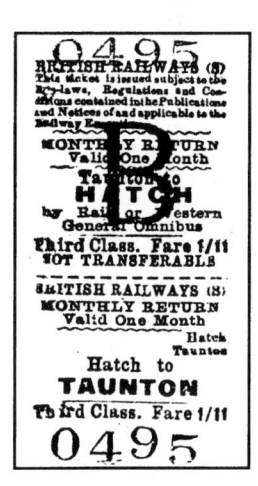

8. The goods yard had a two and a half ton crane and was closed on 6th July 1964. The signal box and goods loop were taken out of use on 23rd September 1956. The village of Hatch Beauchamp had only 470 inhabitants in the 1960s. The main buildings and yard were in commercial use in the 1990s. (Lens of Sutton)

ILTON HALT

9. The halt opened on 26th May 1928 and served a much larger community than Hatch. In the background is a World War II defensive "pill box", with a gun slit visible. (Lens of Sutton)

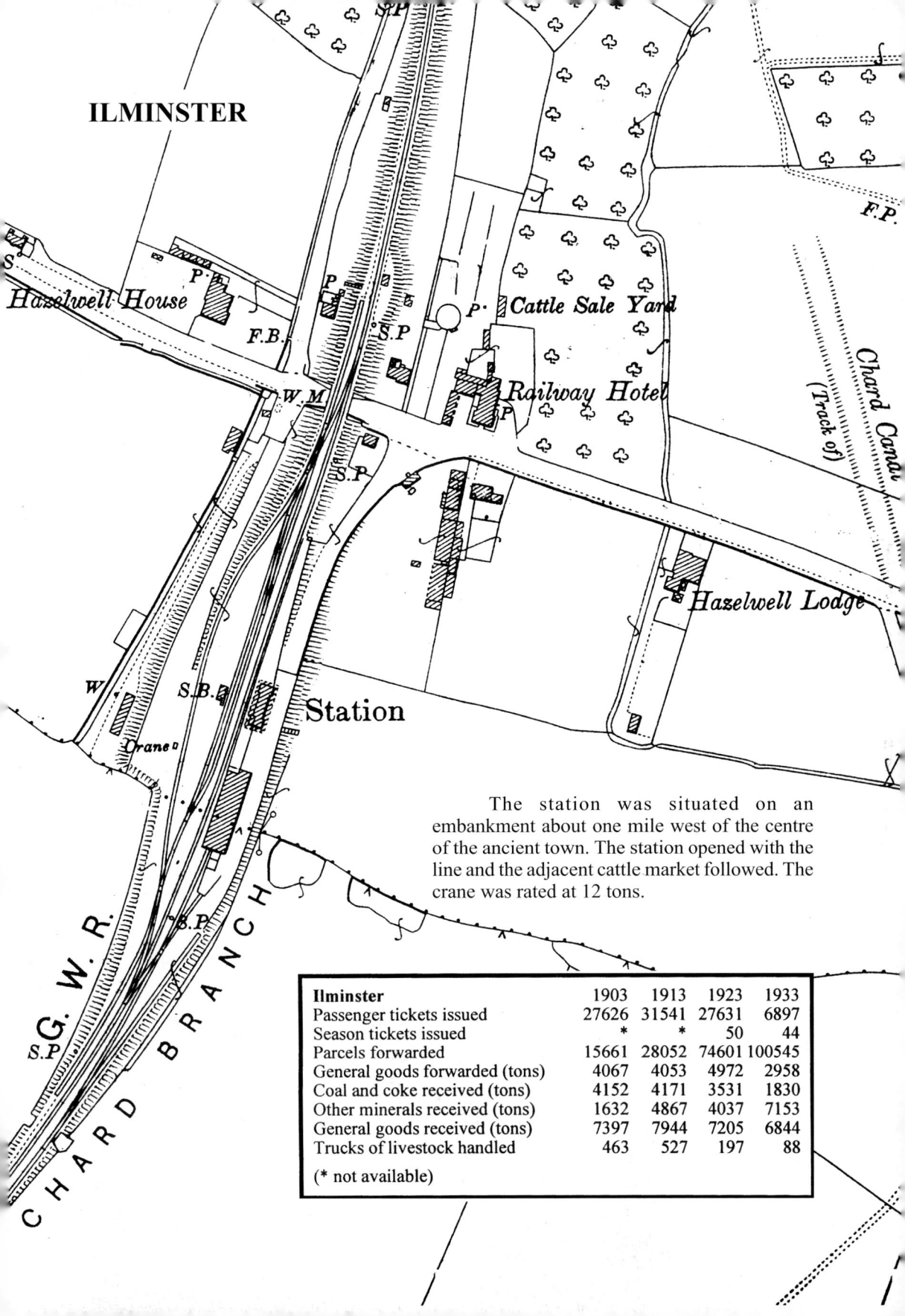

ILMINSTER

The station was situated on an embankment about one mile west of the centre of the ancient town. The station opened with the line and the adjacent cattle market followed. The crane was rated at 12 tons.

Ilminster	1903	1913	1923	1933
Passenger tickets issued	27626	31541	27631	6897
Season tickets issued	*	*	50	44
Parcels forwarded	15661	28052	74601	100545
General goods forwarded (tons)	4067	4053	4972	2958
Coal and coke received (tons)	4152	4171	3531	1830
Other minerals received (tons)	1632	4867	4037	7153
General goods received (tons)	7397	7944	7205	6844
Trucks of livestock handled	463	527	197	88

(* not available)

10. We look south in the 1930s at the slopes of Herne Hill. The main buildings are similar to those at Hatch, although the goods shed was longer. Company and privately owned wagons add variety to the scene; milk vans stand near the signal box, which had 25 levers. (Mowat coll.)

11. The shadow lengthens on the 6.45pm from Taunton, which was worked by no. 9670 on 14th June 1962. The shed on the right was for goods conveyed by passenger train. The main building survived into the 1990s. (R.C.Riley)

12. The signal box and goods yard both ceased to be used on 6th July 1964. The fine arched doorways and elegant gas lamps would soon beecome redundant. It had never been possible to pass two passenger trains here. (Lens of Sutton)

DONYATT HALT

13.   The 5.04pm Chard Junction to Taunton train is about to stop on 8th September 1962. The halt opened on 5th May 1928, its timber structure remaining to the end. No. 4663 has just passed Ilminster distant signal. (C.L.Caddy)

Chard	1903	1913	1923	1933
Passenger tickets issued	25901	27259	24782	7434
Season tickets issued	*	*	228	53
Parcels forwarded	25000	19553	22818	22834
General goods forwarded (tons)	1828	2119	3148	873
Coal and coke received (tons)	2732	1891	1790	1513
Other minerals received (tons)	2283	4005	2566	2448
General goods received (tons)	4012	5301	6960	7189
Trucks of livestock handled	204	149	259	194

(* not available)

Gt. Western Ry.   Gt. Western Ry.
CHARD   CHARD
(R.P.)   TO   (R)
MANCHESTER EXCHANGE
via Severn Tunnel, Hereford, Shrewsbury
and Wrexham
18/2 PARLY.(THIRD CLASS) 18/2
Issued subject to the conditions & regulations set
out in the Company's Time Tables Books and Bills
Manchester Exchange   Manchester Exchange

190

2nd · SINGLE   SINGLE · 2nd
Chard Central to
Chard Central   Chard Central
Chard Junction   Chard Junction
CHARD JUNCTION
(W)   10d. Fare 10d.   (W)
For conditions see over For conditions see over

7073   7073

16. The GWR engine shed (left) was closed on 14th July 1924 and the roof was removed to avoid rates, but the water tank remained in place to be photographed on 23rd August 1958. A Chard Junction to Taunton train is waiting to resume its northward journey from the bay platform, while one bound for the junction stands at the through platform. (A.E.Bennett)

17. The spectacles of two starting signals are visible as ex-GWR class 4500 no. 5504 is ready to leave for the junction. The panelling to the right of the glassless gas lantern bears an inverted V; this is evidence of a canopy that once covered the platform in the foreground and gave protection to LSWR passengers whose trains used a bay on the left; the roof and rails were removed in 1928. (Lens of Sutton)

18. The arched east wall and the smoke ventilators of the elegant train shed become evident in this April 1962 view. The chimney stacks are not original. Having been closed due to the effect of road transport, ironically the building and shed became servants of it, being converted to a tyre centre and still serving as such in the 1990s. (C.L.Caddy)

19. The yard was closed to general goods traffic on 3rd February 1964. Ex-GWR 0-6-0PT no. 3787 slows to allow the driver to surrender the single line staff on 24th June 1962. The signal post built from two rails shows Southern Region influence. The final passenger carrying train from Taunton was the "Quantock Flyer" railtour on 12th February 1964. The 33-lever box closed on 28th July 1964. (R.C.Riley)

20. An April 1965 photograph shows the site in use as the bitumen distribution depot of Lion Emulsions Ltd. Molasses also arrived by rail for B.G.Wyatt Ltd, which used it in animal feed. Their private siding was installed in February 1960 and was a continuation of the one passing through the goods shed. All traffic ceased on 3rd October 1966. Back in 1960, there had been a station master with eight men. (C.L.Caddy)

CHARD TOWN GOODS

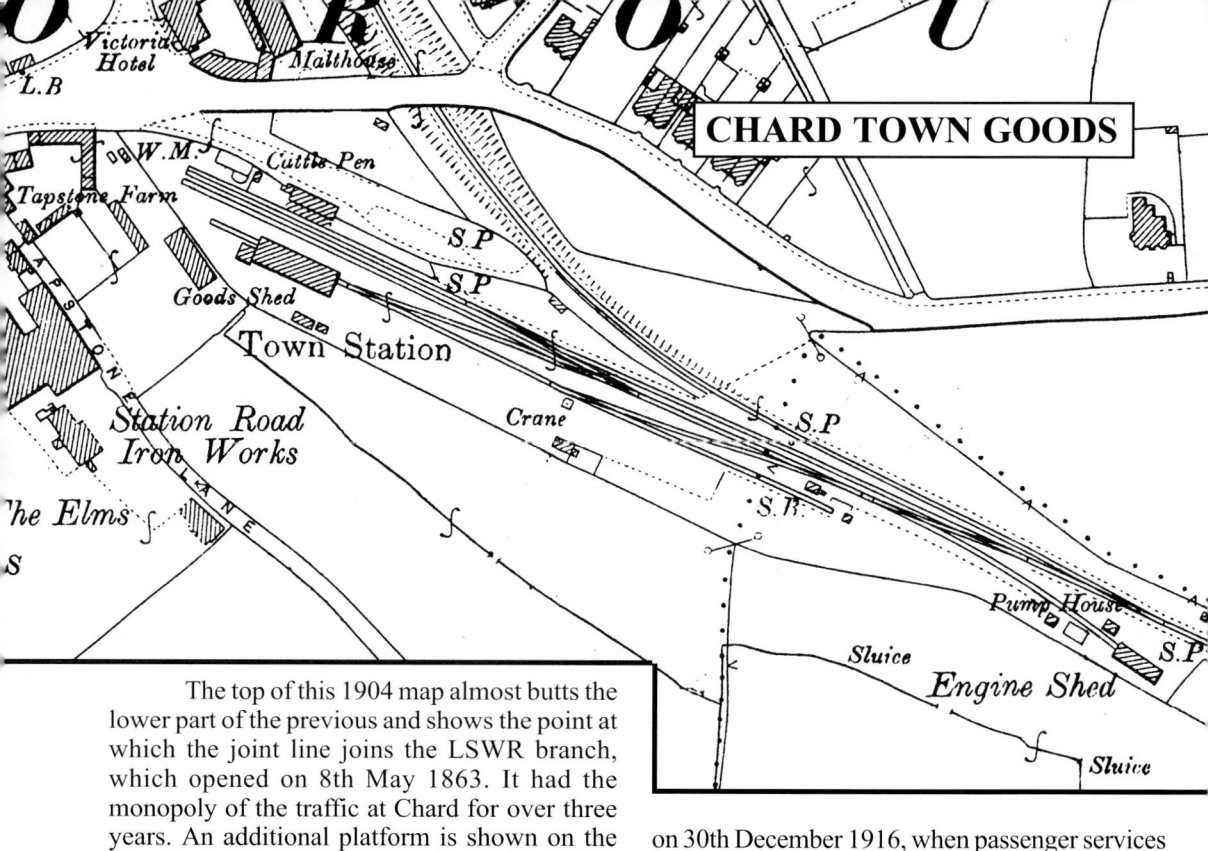

The top of this 1904 map almost butts the lower part of the previous and shows the point at which the joint line joins the LSWR branch, which opened on 8th May 1863. It had the monopoly of the traffic at Chard for over three years. An additional platform is shown on the curve; this came into use in 1871 and was for the benefit of the residents of Old Town. The signal box (S.B.) was replaced by a ground frame on 30th December 1916, when passenger services to the terminus ceased. An extra siding was laid in 1905, this running into Hockey's premises for many years.

21. The stonework of the platform face shows evidence of lengthening. The terminus was known locally as "Tin Station", on account of its corrugated iron cladding. Trains had to be backed out of the station for the engine to run round. (Lens of Sutton)

22. Photographed in 1961, the sign proclaimed the joint operation whch had taken place since 1916 at this location. Beyond the shed was a 5-ton crane, which was supplemented by a mobile crane in the final years. There was a staff of eight in 1960. (J.Scrace)

23. The LSWR engine shed had been in the distance on the right. It was in use until 1916 and was demolished in 1929. Note the coal staithes on the platform in this picture from 30th May 1966; the yard had officially closed on 18th April of that year, but wagons remained awaiting collection. (C.L.Caddy)

CHARD JUNCTION

Chard Road

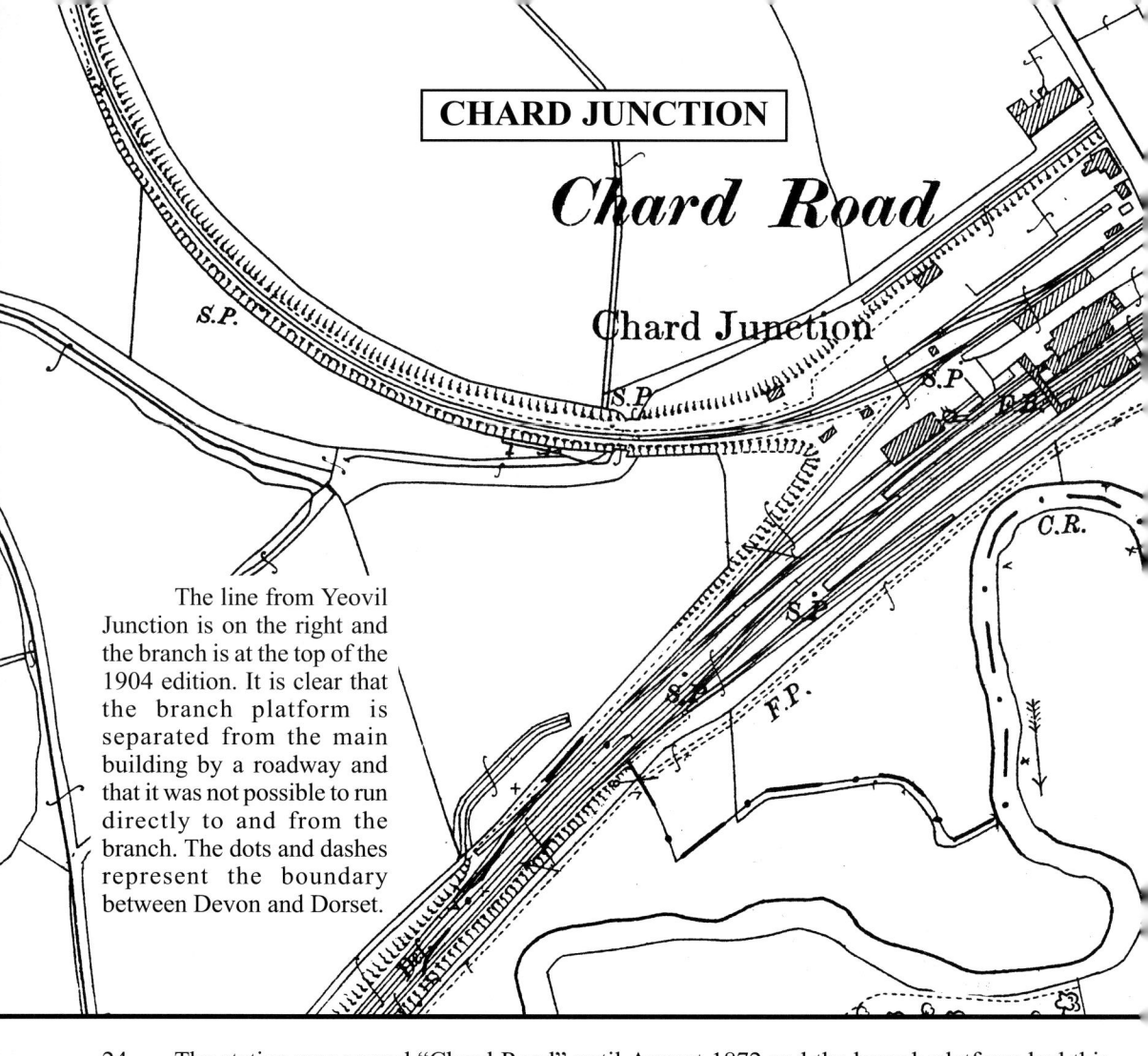

Chard Junction

The line from Yeovil Junction is on the right and the branch is at the top of the 1904 edition. It is clear that the branch platform is separated from the main building by a roadway and that it was not possible to run directly to and from the branch. The dots and dashes represent the boundary between Devon and Dorset.

24. The station was named "Chard Road" until August 1872 and the branch platform had this spacious canopy until the mid-1950s. The fireman is about to uncouple his 4500 class 2-6-2T before running round the train. (Lens of Sutton)

25. The signal box at the end of the curve functioned as a ground frame after 5th March 1935. It is seen from the main line footbridge as no. 3787 arrives from Taunton on 15th June 1962. The goods yard remained in use until 18th April 1966, but the box ceased to be used after 28th July 1964. (R.C.Riley)

For other views of this station, see the companion album *Yeovil to Exeter*, picture nos. 26 to 34.

26. No. 3787 was photographed a few minutes later, together with the Chard Road Hotel and the front of the station building, which was not used by passengers after 7th April 1966 and was demolished in the 1980s. (R.C.Riley)

2. Durston to Yeovil

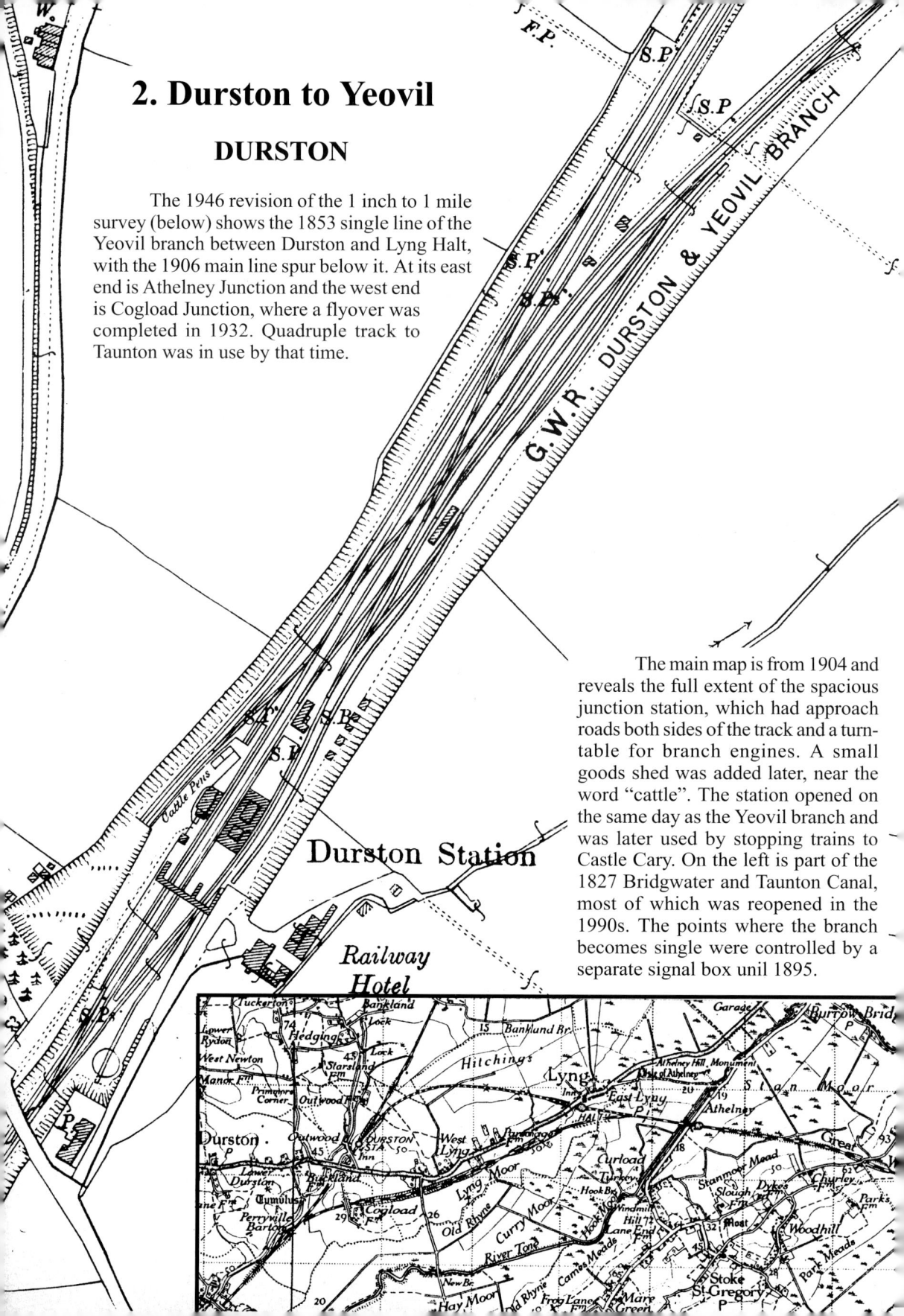

DURSTON

The 1946 revision of the 1 inch to 1 mile survey (below) shows the 1853 single line of the Yeovil branch between Durston and Lyng Halt, with the 1906 main line spur below it. At its east end is Athelney Junction and the west end is Cogload Junction, where a flyover was completed in 1932. Quadruple track to Taunton was in use by that time.

The main map is from 1904 and reveals the full extent of the spacious junction station, which had approach roads both sides of the track and a turntable for branch engines. A small goods shed was added later, near the word "cattle". The station opened on the same day as the Yeovil branch and was later used by stopping trains to Castle Cary. On the left is part of the 1827 Bridgwater and Taunton Canal, most of which was reopened in the 1990s. The points where the branch becomes single were controlled by a separate signal box unil 1895.

27. A 1934 northward panorama from the footbridge has the single line, on which we continue our journey, curving right beyond the massive 71-lever signal box, which was opened in 1895. The staff seem busy, as cattle wagons stand in the up siding. The shed in the distance was for the Permanent Way Dept. (LGRP/NRM)

28. Looking south in 1956, we can spot the small goods shed beyond the cattle pens. The lamp silhouetted against the footbridge was to illuminate the single line tablet pick up arm. Closure came in 1964, when goods traffic ended on 6th July and passenger trains ceased to call on 5th October. (H.C.Casserley)

LYNG HALT

29. The short halt was opened on 24th September 1928 and was photographed on 8th December 1963. It was closed a few months before Durston, on 15th June 1964, as it was served only by Yeovil trains at that time. It was close to the village of East Lyng. (C.L.Caddy)

ATHELNEY

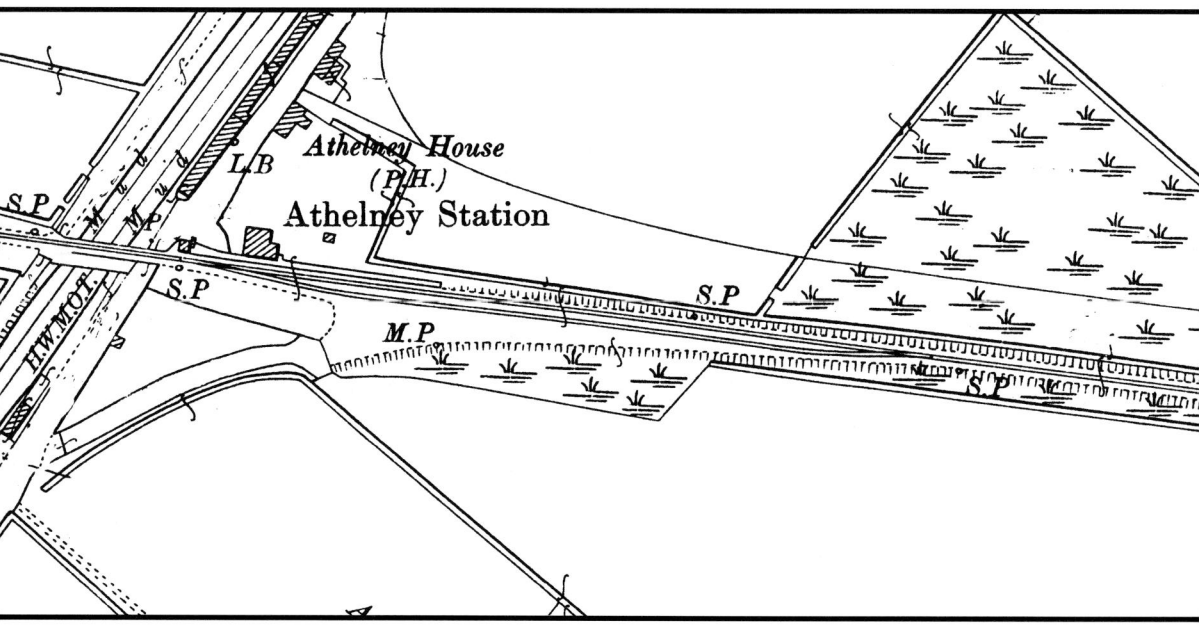

The 1904 edition indicates the position of the goods siding and signal box before the track was doubled.

30. This signal box was in use from 1881 until 1906 and had a 14-lever frame. Visible through the gates is the bridge over the River Tone. The "S" plate indicated that the signal lineman was required; a "T" on a diamond referred to the telegraph engineer. (Lens of Sutton)

31. A new box with 37 levers was built on the opposite side of the track in 1908. The buildings were erected at the same time and are seen in the 1950s. They ceased to be used when the branch closed but goods traffic continued for another month, ceasing on 6th July 1964. (Lens of Sutton)

32. A westward view includes the two goods sidings and the 30cwt capacity crane. The centre signal was for the main line, the one on the right was for the single line to Durston and on the left is the one for the down goods loop, which was in place from 1943 to 1979. The box closed on 4th April 1986. (Lens of Sutton)

EAST OF ATHELNEY

33. After travelling for nearly three miles, mainly across West Sedge Moor, our train reaches Curry Rivel Junction and passes behind the signal box as it starts its journey down the branch. It was built in 1906 (with a 41-lever frame) when the line to Langport West was doubled and the new line through Langport East to Castle Cary was opened. There was a goods loop on the other side of the train, which is bound for Athelney. (C.L.Caddy)

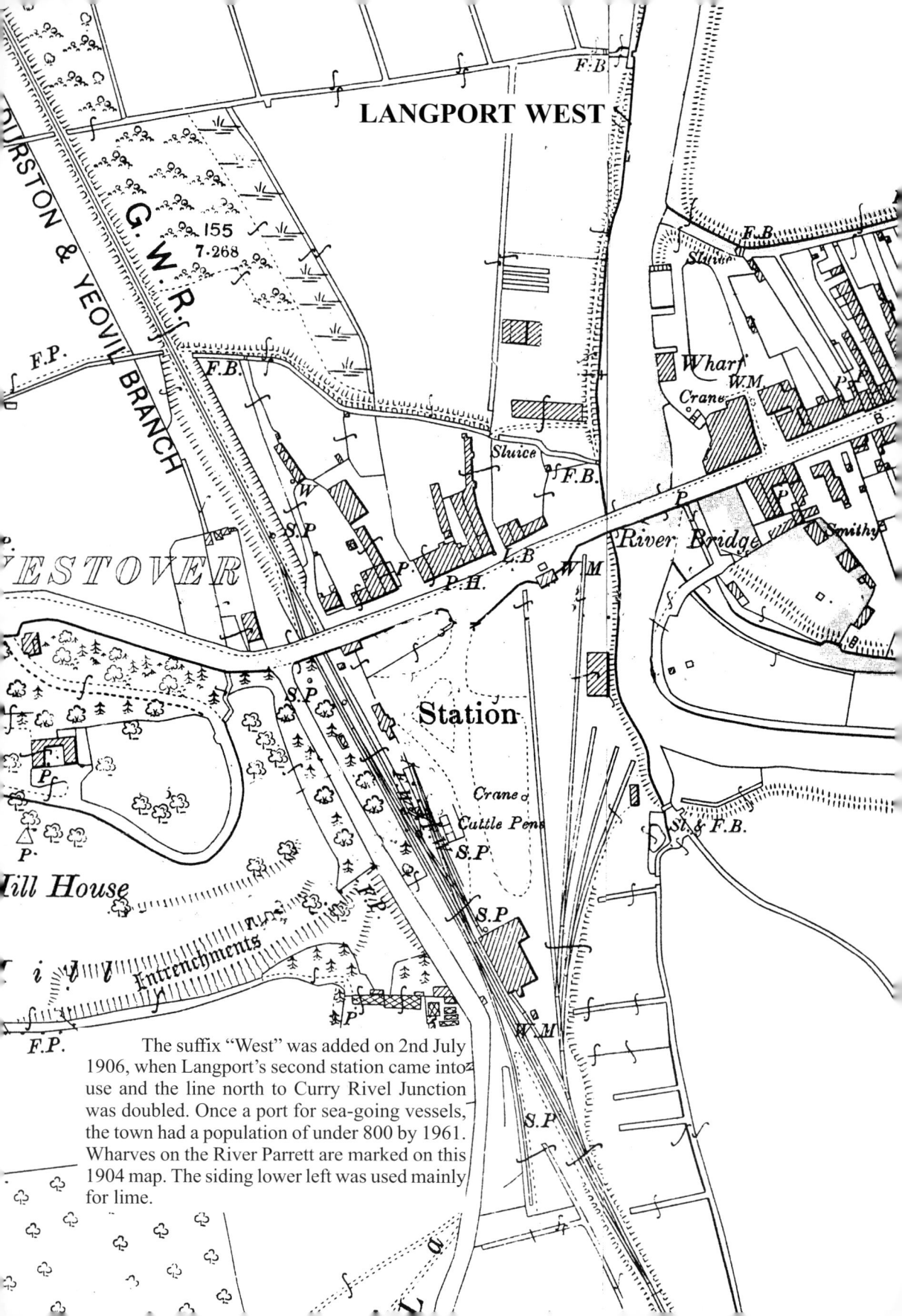

LANGPORT WEST

The suffix "West" was added on 2nd July 1906, when Langport's second station came into use and the line north to Curry Rivel Junction was doubled. Once a port for sea-going vessels, the town had a population of under 800 by 1961. Wharves on the River Parrett are marked on this 1904 map. The siding lower left was used mainly for lime.

34. A photograph from November 1894 shows the position of the signal box until 1906 - note the plea for help as both letters are displayed by the signalman. (Lens of Sutton)

35. Further flooding occurred in December 1910 and on many occasions subsequently. A bowler hat is projected carefully from the footplate of no. 11, an Armstrong 388 class in charge of a milk van and four four-wheelers. (Lens of Sutton)

36. The wide space between the tracks is a legacy of the broad gauge era, as is the space to the left of the cattle wagons. Trailing connections to the goods yard were in the interest of safety. A siding for the War Department was laid beyond the bridge, on the east side, and was in place from 1940-1947. (Lens of Sutton)

37. Looking south we see the 1906 signal box, with the tablet catcher at the end of the platform and the lime siding, which was provided on 22nd August 1885 for Mead & Son. Goods traffic ceased on 6th July 1964. (Lens of Sutton)

Langport West	1903	1913	1923	1933
Passenger tickets issued	28191	30376	16611	12506
Season tickets issued	*	*	45	150
Parcels forwarded	27255	24619	60222	42635
General goods forwarded (tons)	7339	5963	6490	3613
Coal and coke received (tons)	7588	3557	1605	671
Other minerals received (tons)	9366	3047	7323	955
General goods received (tons)	12557	7271	6152	3597
Trucks of livestock handled	927	759	644	292

(* not available)

38. A July 1962 record reveals the solid styling employed on the branch - there are even some stone mullions. There was a staff of 16 to 19 men throughout the 1930s, although traffic was in decline. (H.C.Casserley)

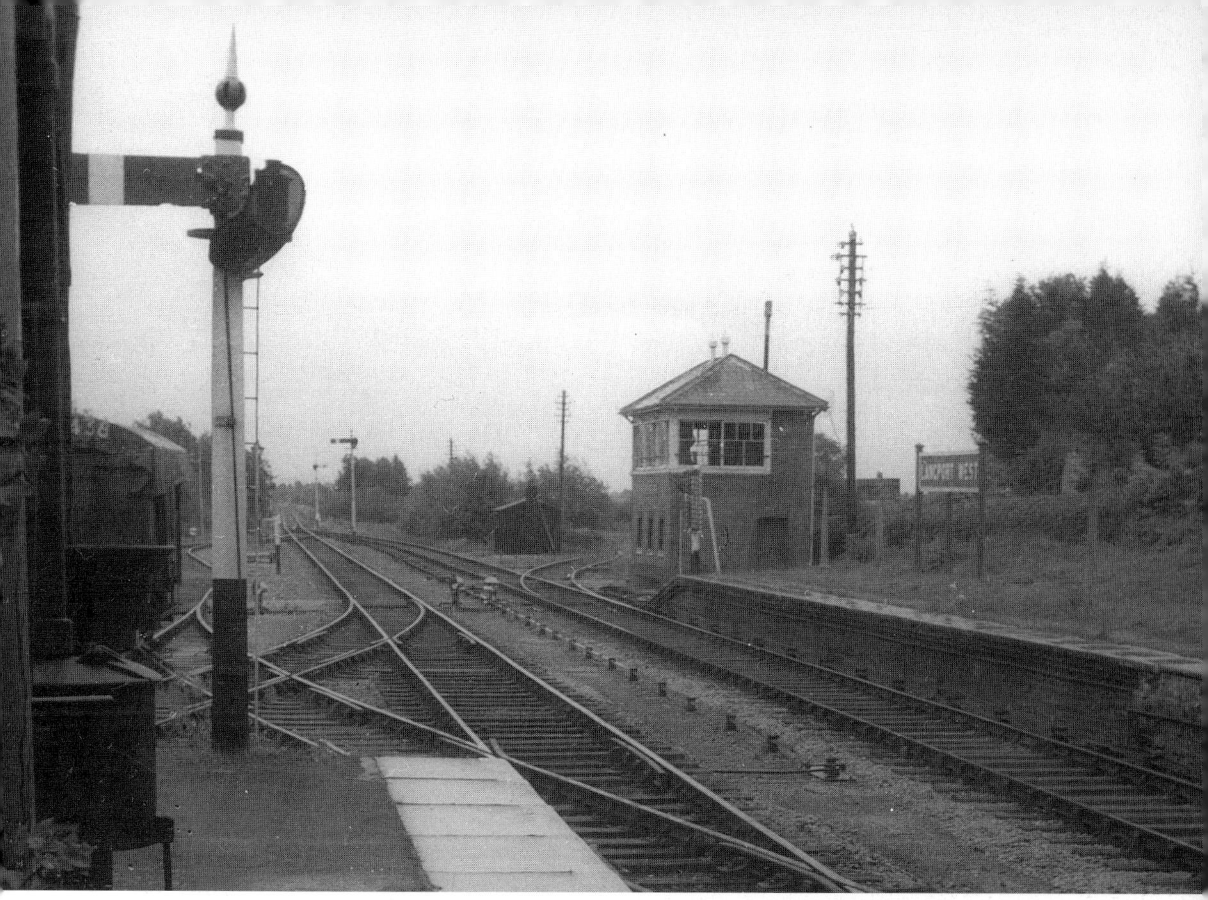

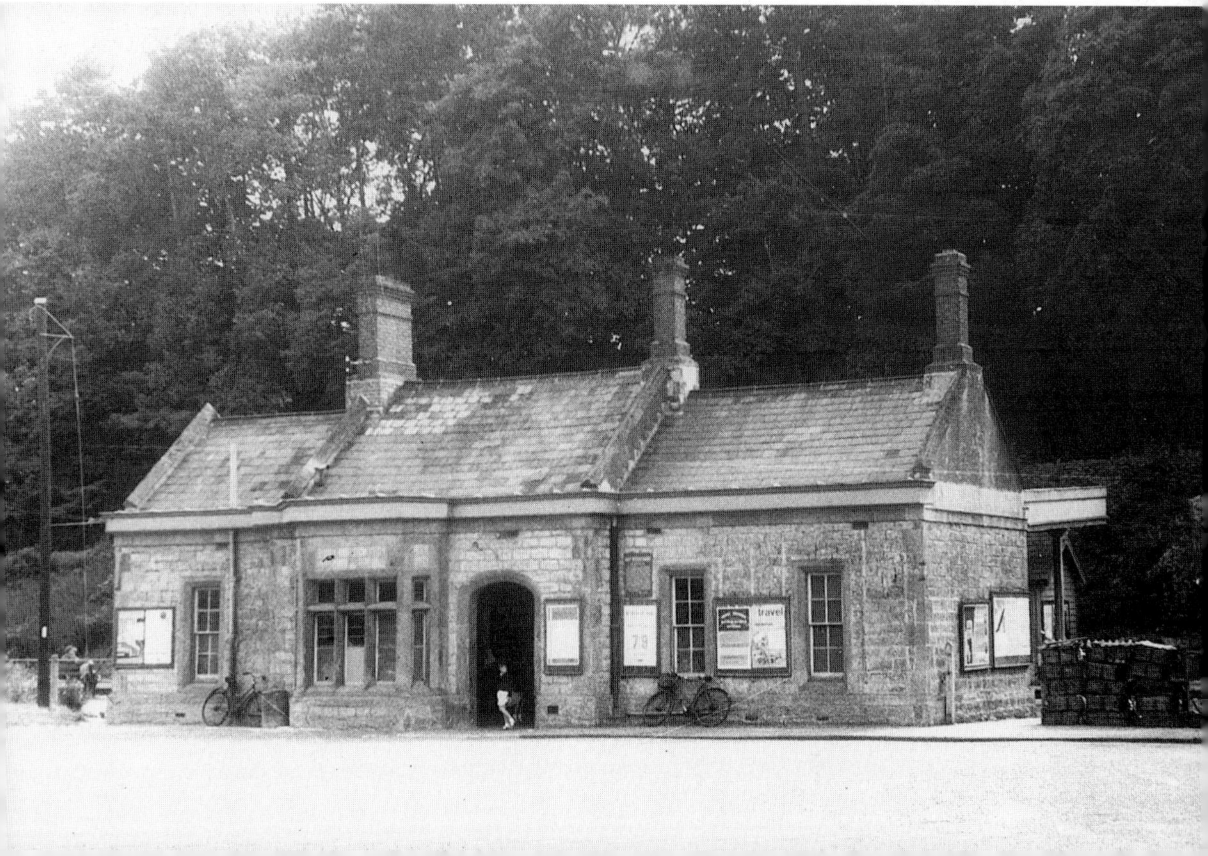
travel

THORNEY AND KINGSBURY HALT

39. The halt was brought into use on 28th November 1927, but there were few dwellings in the vicinity. It was more than one mile north of Kingsbury Episcopi. There was a small office at the far end of the building, which was photographed in 1962. (C.L.Caddy)

40. In the background of the photograph above is the siding featured here. It was provided on 21st November 1932 for the Nestle and Anglo Swiss Condensed Milk Company and is seen in this northward panorama in 1964. One oil lamp was throughtfully provided for nocturnal shunting. (J.H.Day)

MARTOCK

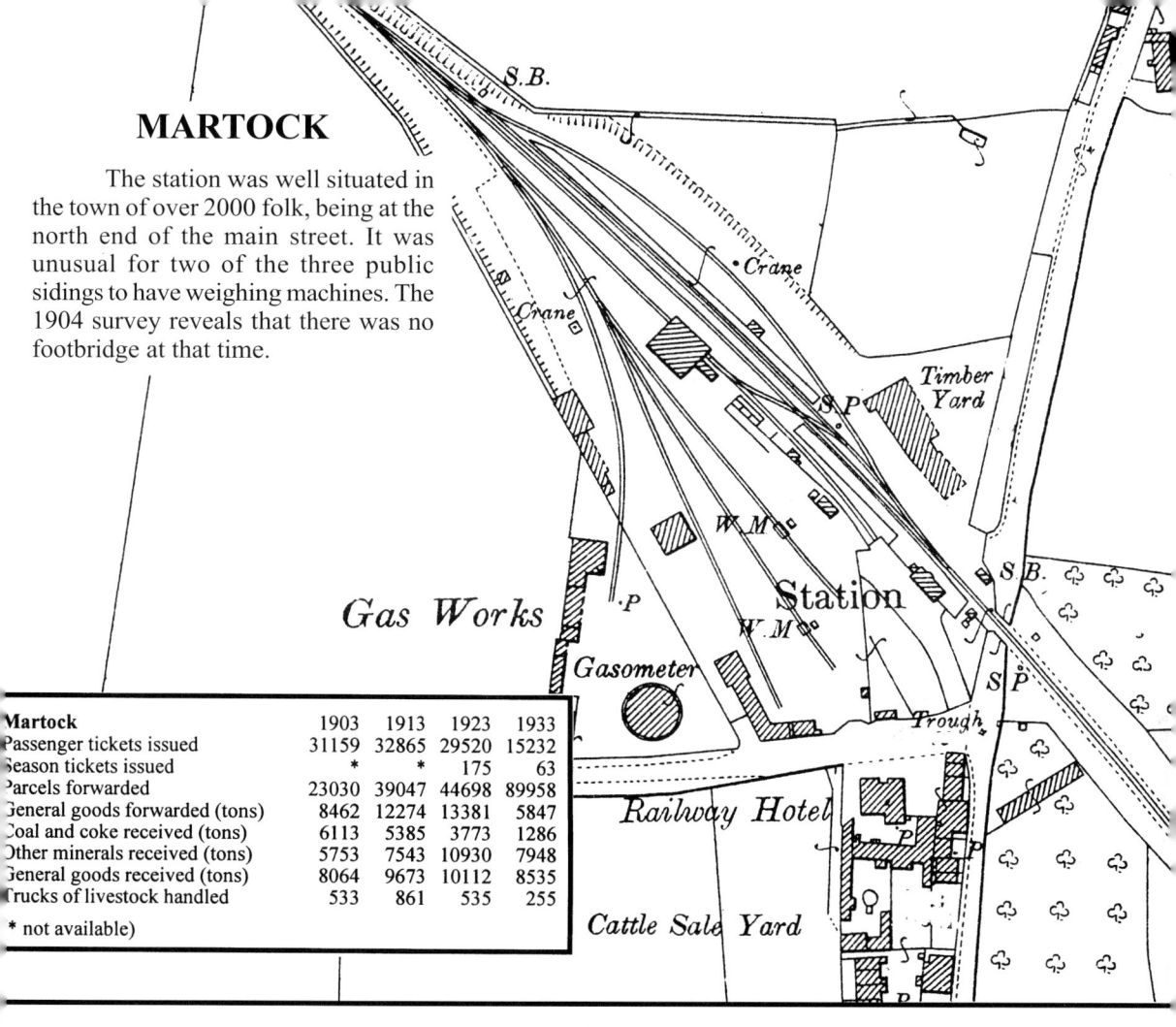

The station was well situated in the town of over 2000 folk, being at the north end of the main street. It was unusual for two of the three public sidings to have weighing machines. The 1904 survey reveals that there was no footbridge at that time.

Martock	1903	1913	1923	1933
Passenger tickets issued	31159	32865	29520	15232
Season tickets issued	*	*	175	63
Parcels forwarded	23030	39047	44698	89958
General goods forwarded (tons)	8462	12274	13381	5847
Coal and coke received (tons)	6113	5385	3773	1286
Other minerals received (tons)	5753	7543	10930	7948
General goods received (tons)	8064	9673	10112	8535
Trucks of livestock handled	533	861	535	255

(* not available)

41. There was a staff of 15 in 1903, this rising to 19 ten years later. This animated scene was recorded by a postcard manufacturer during that era and includes a gas lamp mounted on a sewer vent pipe. The signal box is thought to date from about 1880. (Lens of Sutton)

42. Here are examples of Edwardian costume, footbridge roof valencing and carriage roof design. The latter was known as clerestory (pronounced clear-story), the extra headroom sometimes being used to accommodate gas lights, which were an improvement on oil. (Lens of Sutton)

43. Probably taken in the 1930s, this view towards Langport includes the shed for goods by passenger train and the crane for the down siding. There was another in the up yard. The bridge was devoid of a roof in the final years. (Lens of Sutton)

44. We now have two views from the footbridge in 1962-63. This one includes cattle wagons, which were soon to disappear from the railway scene altogether. The point rods and signal wires certainly take a tortuous course. (C.L.Caddy)

45. Passenger trains often passed here but the staggered platforms made their photography difficult. We witness the arrival of a train from Taunton behind 2-6-2T no. 4593 and note that the goods yard is grass covered, although it remained open until 6th July 1964. Refrigerated meat vans were loaded here for many years. (J.W.T.House/C.L.Caddy)

MONTACUTE

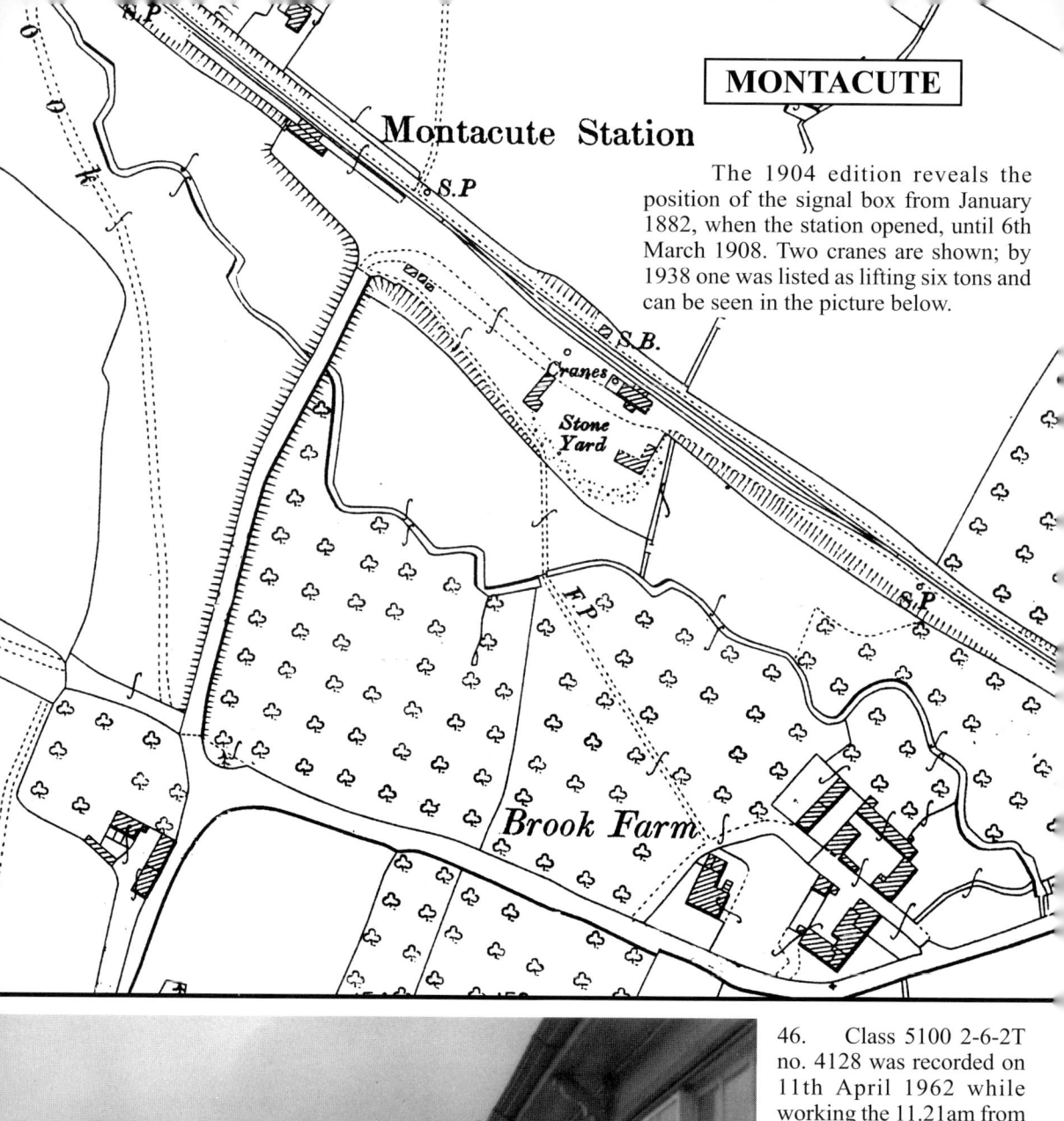

The 1904 edition reveals the position of the signal box from January 1882, when the station opened, until 6th March 1908. Two cranes are shown; by 1938 one was listed as lifting six tons and can be seen in the picture below.

46. Class 5100 2-6-2T no. 4128 was recorded on 11th April 1962 while working the 11.21am from Yeovil Pen Mill to Taunton. Goods facilities were withdrawn on 30th September 1963 and the siding was soon lifted. The upper quadrant signal replaced a bomb damaged GWR one in December 1950 but the box had been switched out, except during shunting, since about 1930. (R.A.Lumber)

47. The prospective passenger's perspective was pictured on 12th July 1962; few saw it as there were only about 800 residents at the time and the village centre was half a mile to the south. The realigned A3088 now occupies the site of the railway for two miles each side of this location. (H.C.Casserley)

Montacute	1903	1913	1923	1933
Passenger tickets issued	14959	16035	16423	4808
Season tickets issued	*	*	70	6
Parcels forwarded	4524	9632	16561	11280
General goods forwarded (tons)	698	1092	387	170
Coal and coke received (tons)	1173	877	667	187
Other minerals received (tons)	2218	2292	2656	2300
General goods received (tons)	625	1035	645	459
Trucks of livestock handled	10	63	4	15

(* not available)

48. The 1906 signal box closed on 8th March 1964, just before this photograph was taken. Note that resleepering was taking place only weeks before closure, not uncommon in those days of drastic cuts. No. 82044 was one the BR class 3 2-6-2Ts introduced to the route in its final months. (Lens of Sutton)

HENDFORD

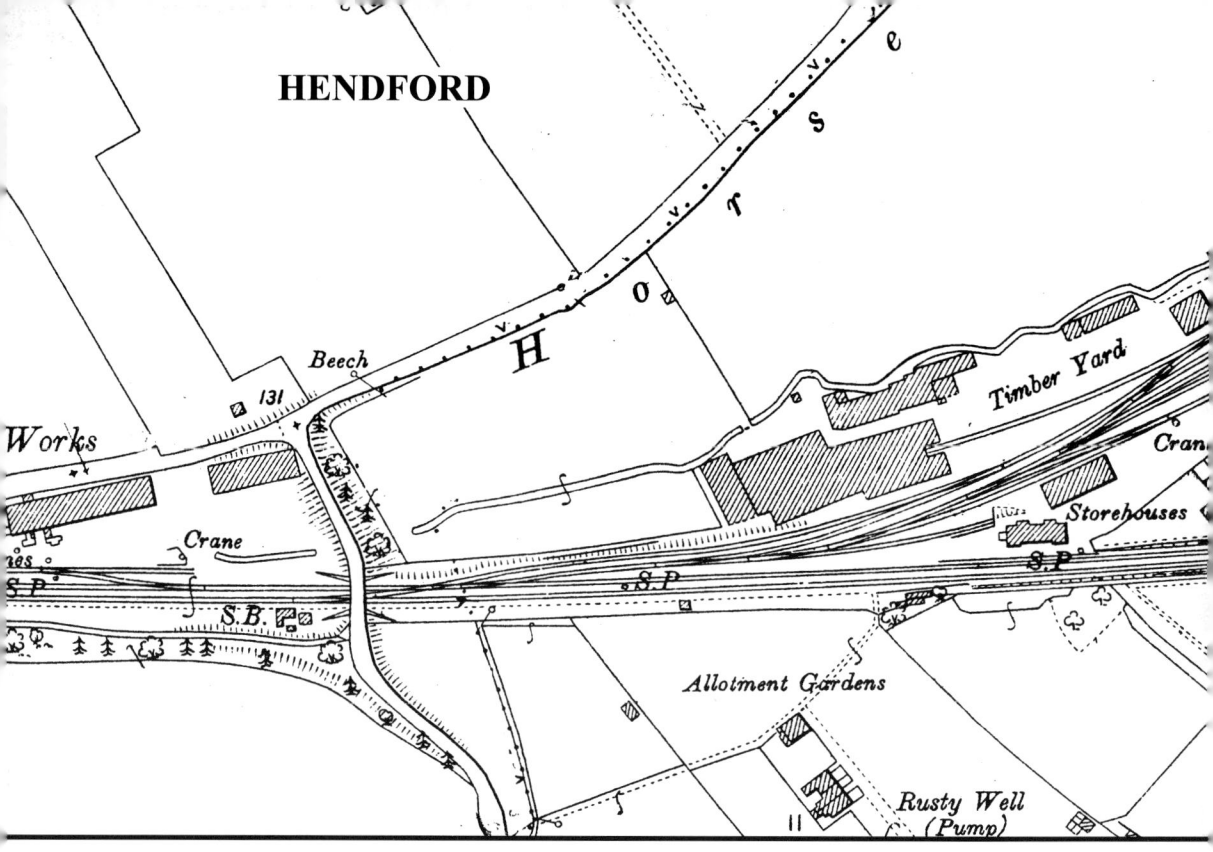

The terminus of the broad gauge branch from Durston, together with an engine shed, was situated here from 26th October 1853 until 2nd February 1857, on which date the line was extended to Pen Mill, right on this 1903 map. The lower line on this side had been laid to standard gauge and was used by LSWR trains from Salisbury to Hendford from 1st June 1860 until 1st June 1861, when Yeovil Town opened. Of the three lines on the left, the centre one is the running line from Montacute, the lower one is a headshunt and the upper one is the siding for the Ham Hill & Doulting Stone Company. Further west there was a siding south of the line from about 1920 to 1960 for Bunford Flax Mill and on the north side for Petters Ltd., manufacturers of oil engines, pumps, generators etc., which came into use on 29th March 1913 and conveyed the traffic of their Westland Aircraft Works until September 1965. Initially they used a Manning Wardle 0-4-0ST for shunting; different diesels were used until the siding closed in May 1968.

Route diagram 1923-43
(Railway Magazine)

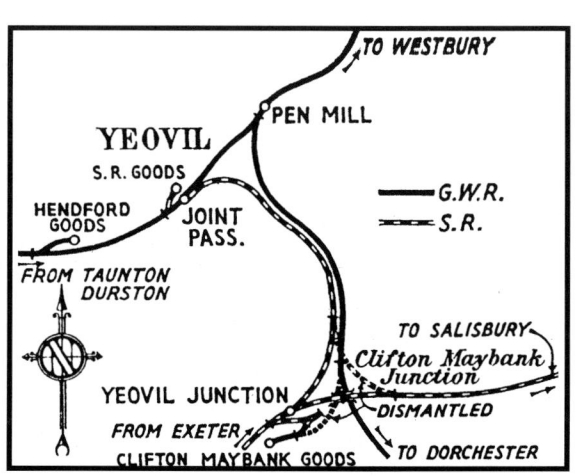

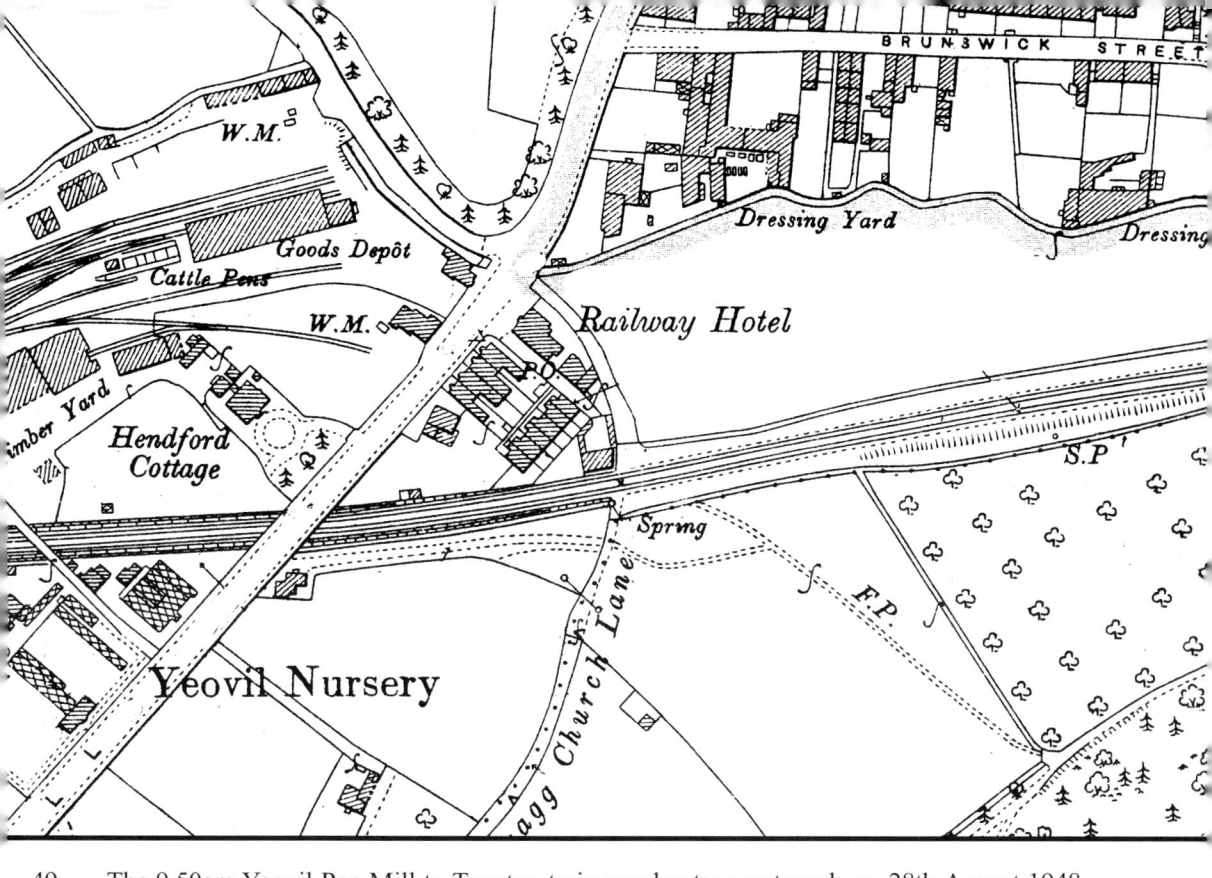

49. The 9.50am Yeovil Pen Mill to Taunton train accelerates westwards on 28th August 1948, while a Taunton to Yeovil freight waits in the siding. The stone works and its siding can be seen through the smoke and steam. (R.A.Lumber)

50. Looking in the other direction from the same bridge, but on 13th August 1961, we see the commencement of the fan of goods sidings as a permanent way train rattles under our feet. In the distance is the 1853 passenger station building. (J.H.Day)

51. A closer look at the 1853 Bristol & Exeter station in 1964 shows it to have been well buttressed subsequently. A Southern Region upper quadrant signal is evident; the distant is fixed and refers to Yeovil Town. On the right is the goods line to that station, where it was used as a carriage siding and headshunt. It was initially the final part of the Salisbury & Yeovil Railway. (J.H.Day)

52. The bridge from which pictures 49 and 50 were taken is featured, along with Hendford Halt, which was opened on 2nd May 1932 to serve the growing industrial district. The signal box closed on 12th September 1965. (C.L.Caddy)

53. No. 4593 is working the 12.37pm from Pen Mill on 13th June 1964, the last day of passenger services. The once busy yard had handled every type of merchandise but traffic dwindled until closure took place on 9th October 1967. The yard had a crane of 10-ton capacity in 1938. (J.H.Day)

WEST OF YEOVIL TOWN

54. Seen from Addlewell Lane bridge on 15th May 1964 is class 22 no. D6331 with the 12.58pm from Taunton to Pen Mill and stock standing on the former SYR line to Hendford. These economical machines were little used on the branch. (J.H.Day)

55. The bridge used for the previous picture is in the background as a DMU leaves the siding to enter the Town station, having waited there for the 11.24am to Taunton to pass on 9th May 1964. It will work to Pen Mill at 11.32, where such units had been a common sight on Weymouth trains since 1959. (J.H.Day)

56. The two tracks in the background of the previous picture are seen from the other direction on 13th October 1966, as no. D4021 proceeds towards Hendford. The siding had been connected to the old running line on 12th September 1965 and the stops were added at that time. (R.A.Lumber)

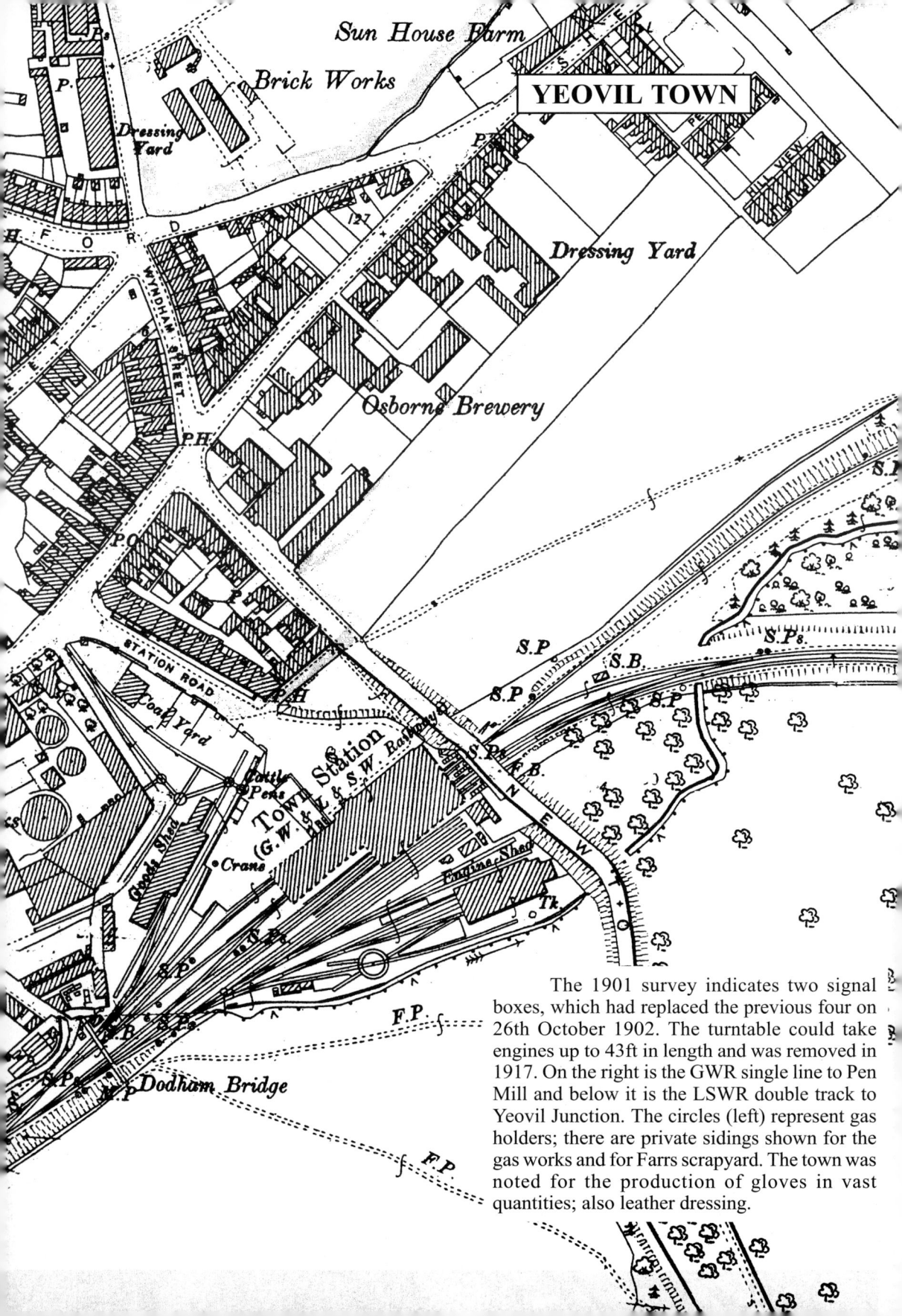

YEOVIL TOWN

The 1901 survey indicates two signal boxes, which had replaced the previous four on 26th October 1902. The turntable could take engines up to 43ft in length and was removed in 1917. On the right is the GWR single line to Pen Mill and below it is the LSWR double track to Yeovil Junction. The circles (left) represent gas holders; there are private sidings shown for the gas works and for Farrs scrapyard. The town was noted for the production of gloves in vast quantities; also leather dressing.

57. The construction was a joint venture between the BER and the LSWR but each supplied its own staff, initially. Signalling was a joint operation after 1882, the GWR having undertaken it previously. The fine symmetrical structure made a bold statement to the town. Later, the building was maintained by the LSWR/SR and the signalling by the GWR. Staffing was a joint operation, uniforms showing "S&GWR". (Lens of Sutton)

58. Most of the goods yard on the left was LSWR property, except for the three sidings nearest to the GWR passenger train. The class O2 0-4-4T is on the line leading to the LSWR engine shed. (R.A.Lumber coll.)

60. A view from about 1930 has the GWR's through line and three sidings on the left. By that date, the SR controlled everything to the right of the island platform. Autocoaches of the type seen on the left were used to Pen Mill and on some stopping services on the Weymouth line. They were based at Weymouth. (Mowat coll.)

61. Waiting to depart for Taunton from the GWR platform is 4500 class 2-6-2T no. 4547. The roof bracing wires are evident in the earlier picture but the smoke hood is a later addition to the elegant structure. (Lens of Sutton)

62. As with the Crystal Palace, which was first erected only ten years prior to this pair of imposing sheds, the cast iron components were very durable but the timber parts supporting the glass were not so. An SR train, headed by a class D1 0-4-2T stands under the failing glazed panel in the mid-1930s. (Lens of Sutton)

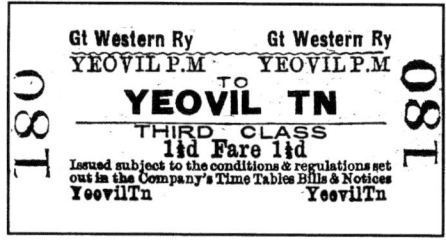

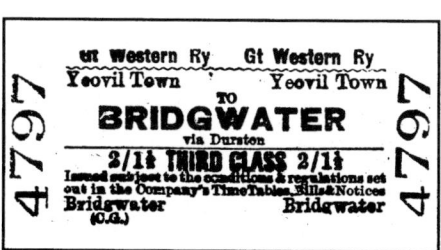

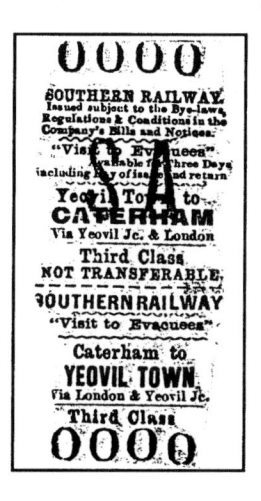

63. The engine shed, the south side of the train shed and one of the two houses built for station masters were photographed on 12th June 1926. At this time, the SR allocated mostly 4-4-0s to its shed here for working between Salisbury and Exeter. The roof was added to the coal stage in 1920. (H.C.Casserley)

64. SR class S11 4-4-0 no. 399 waits to leave for the Junction, where it will probably run round its train and continue to Salisbury. On the right is a GWR clerestory-roofed train with a tank wagon and vans in tow. Work is in progress following removal of the roof in the early 1930s. (Lens of Sutton)

65. Other details of the intricate stone quoins became evident after the demolition of the train shed, but few would have appreciated them on a wet day. The platform was low in relation to the floor of the SR train, a disadvantage when loading milk churns and other heavy commodities. (Lens of Sutton)

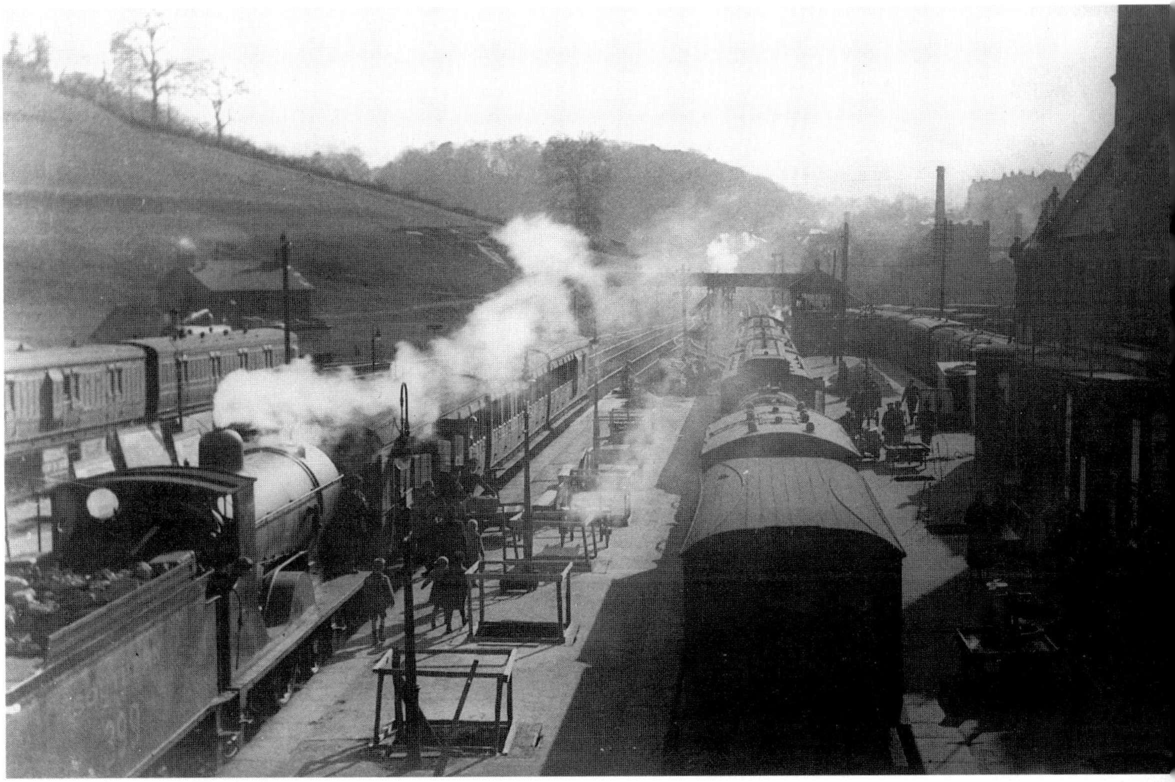

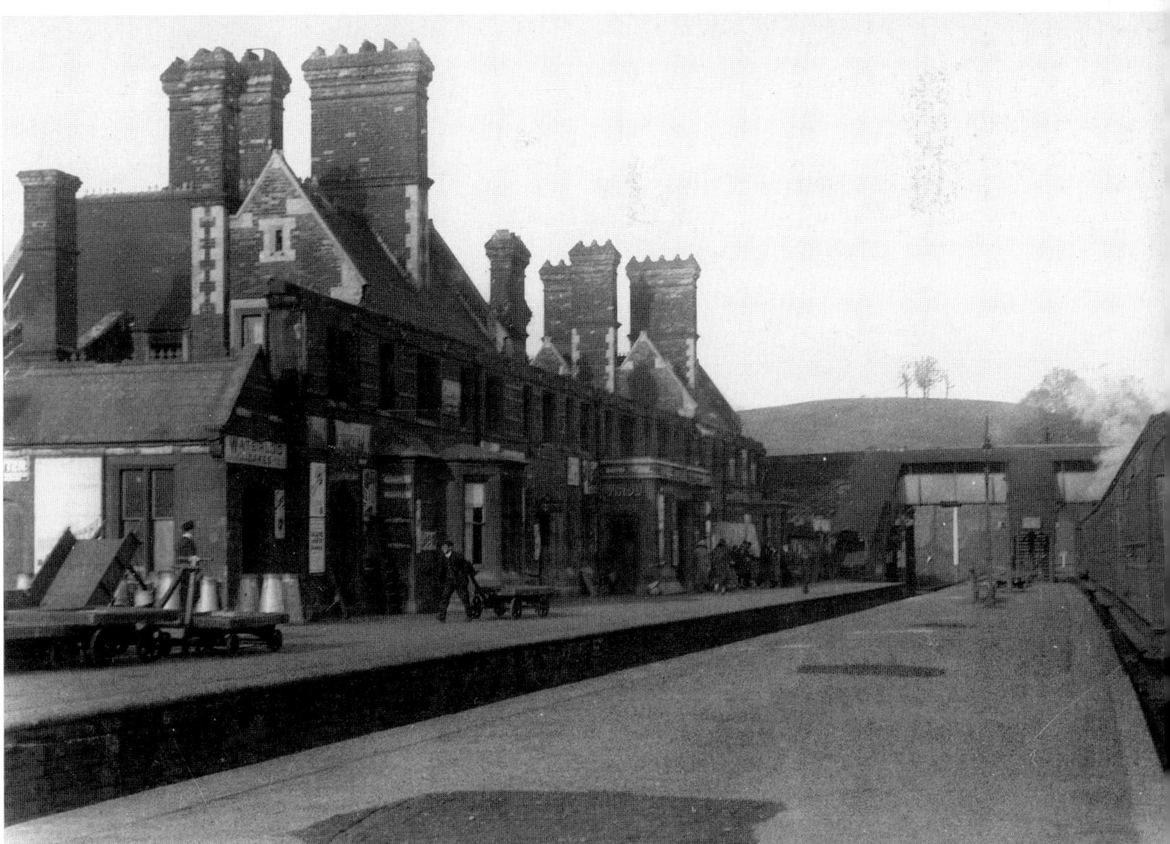

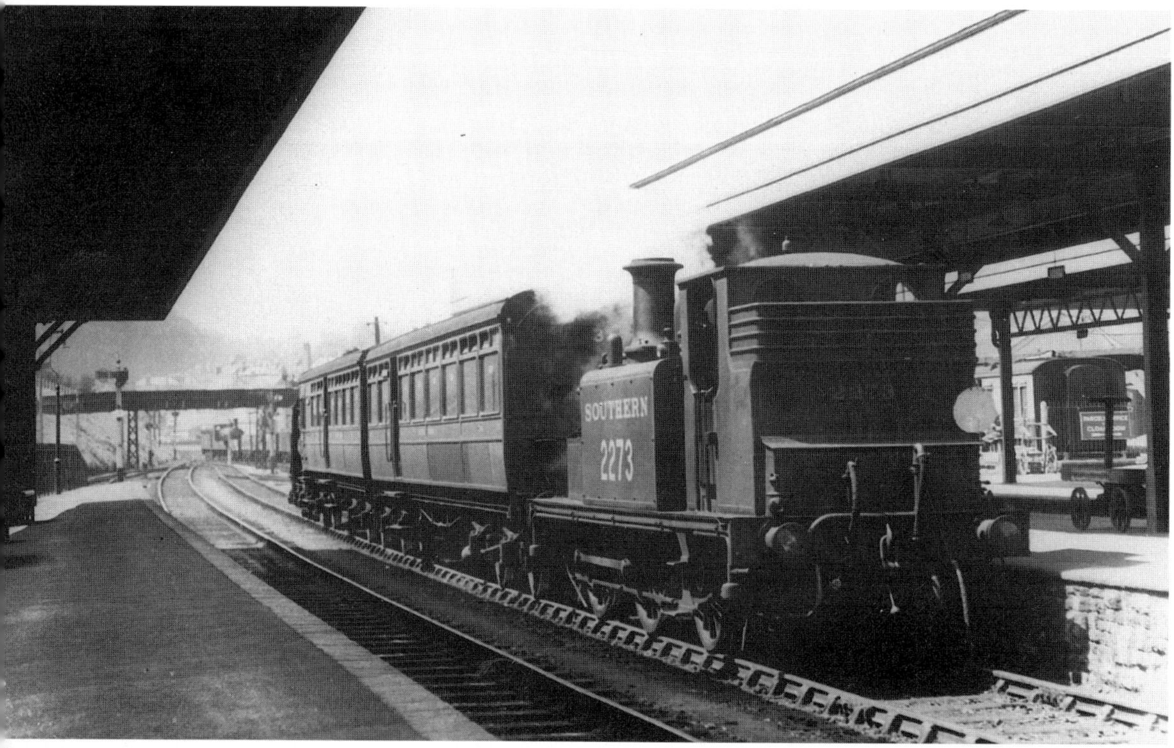
SOUTHERN
2273

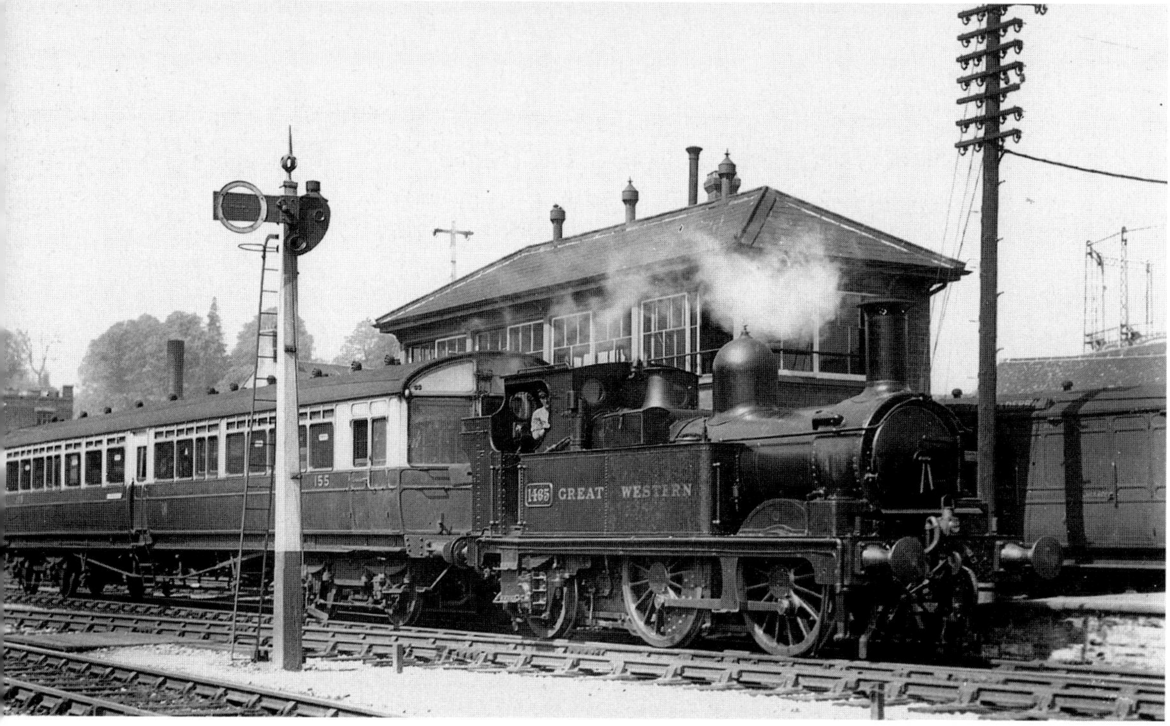
155
1465 GREAT WESTERN

66. Individual platform canopies of the SR style were eventually erected, these being largely constructed of steel. A goods train is across the Taunton line while a Brighton-built class D1 0-4-2T no. 2273 waits with a train for the Junction on 21st May 1935. (H.C.Casserley)

67. The GWR was also employing an 0-4-2T on the same day for its local service to Pen Mill. It is no. 1465 of the 517 class, built in 1883. The tapered wooden signal post carries a shunt signal, which has small spectacle glasses to distinguish it from other signals. (H.C.Casserley)

68. Between the engine shed (left) and the siding where the coaches are standing were four sidings. Under the hoist on 13th August 1946 is class B4 0-4-0T no. 94, probably returning to its home shed at Plymouth Friary after overhaul at Eastleigh. Also visible is part of the resident breakdown train. (Wessex coll.)

73. A panorama from 30th July 1961 includes the full length of all the platform canopies and the short one with partial side screen for the dock siding, which was used for mail and parcel traffic. On the right is the 1959 water tank and the single storey enginemens mess room, which was always full of tobacco smoke and debate. (E.W.Fry)

Closure summary

15-6-1964	Passengers to Taunton
6-7-1964	Goods to Taunton
3-5-1965	Local goods
29-11-1965	Passengers to Pen Mill
2-10-1966	Passengers to Junction
1-3-1967	Local parcels (Line to Junc. closed then)
9-10-1967	Goods to Hendford
6-5-1968	Freight to Westlands

74. Arriving with the 4.05pm from Pen Mill on 10th July 1962 is 0-6-0PT no. 9732. It is passing the lower quadrant down main home, while the upper quadrant down Southern starter is also off. The signal on the right was stunted because of the limited clearance. (H.C.Casserley)

75. Royal Blue Coaches deprived the railway of many passengers and ironically loaded their vehicles in the forecourt, but the refreshment room benefitted. Here is one of the most imposing buildings in the town and certainly the most significant in its commercial history but the Town Council chose to demolish it after acquiring it in 1970. This and the next picture were taken in 1963. (C.L.Caddy)

76. The three passenger lines were known as Main, Down Southern and Up Southern; a van train is shunting from the latter on 23rd March 1963. By that date the shed allocation included mainly ex-SR class U 2-6-0s, plus some ex-GWR 0-4-2Ts, 2-6-2Ts and 0-6-0PTs. "Battle of Britain" and "West Country" Pacifics together with some BR types were regular visitors. (C.L.Caddy)

77. Ex-GWR class 4500s were still working in 1964; no. 4593 leaves at 4.8pm for the 59- minute run to Taunton. The 55-lever signal box was in use from 15th October 1916 to 1st March 1967. (M.J.Messenger)

78. Several former GWR engines appeared here after Pen Mill shed was closed in January 1959. On shed at noon on Sunday 16th May 1965 were nos. D808, 75007, 9754, 75005, 41283, 41290, 80039, 82035 and 80035. Steam vanished from this scene on 12th June 1965. (R.A.Lumber)

79. A photograph from 5th July 1965 shows that the depot continued to be used for the stabling of diesels, a DMU, a "Warship" class and a railbus being on view on this weekday. The cranes, both steam and water, stand silent for ever, but stabling continued until 1968. (M.J.Messenger)

80. For long after official closure, the site was used for the reception of track materials lifted during the singling of the Castle Cary to Dorchester route. This is the melancholy scene on 1st September 1969. (R.A.Lumber)

3. Castle Cary to Yeovil Junction

CASTLE CARY

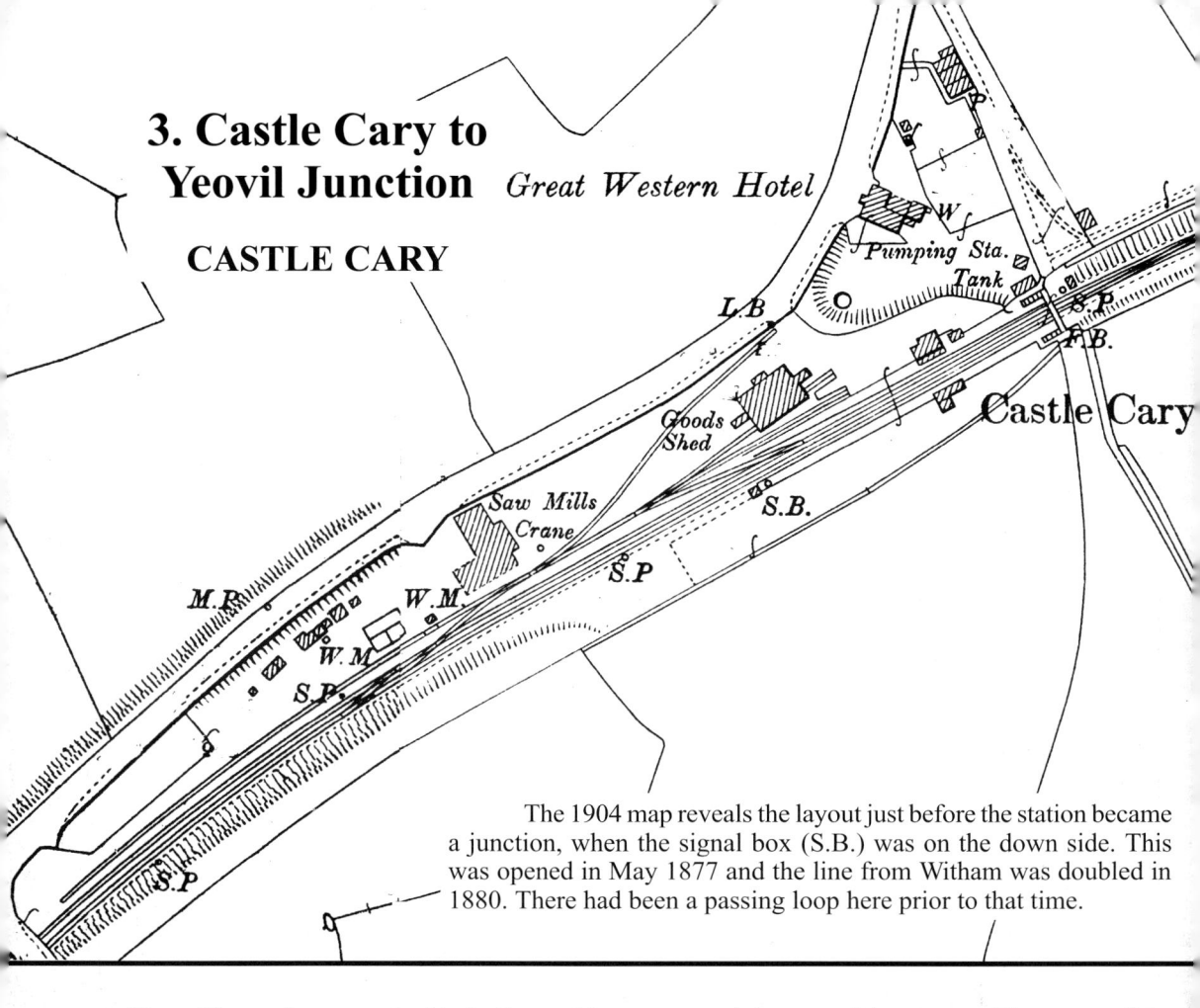

The 1904 map reveals the layout just before the station became a junction, when the signal box (S.B.) was on the down side. This was opened in May 1877 and the line from Witham was doubled in 1880. There had been a passing loop here prior to that time.

81. The station opened with the line and is seen around the turn of the century. The centre of the hill top town is nearly one mile to the south. It had a population of about 1800 by 1960. (Lens of Sutton)

82. When the line to Taunton (left) was built, the connection to the goods yard was moved westwards and a new 55-lever signal box (centre) was provided. Our route to Yeovil is in the foreground of this 1922 photograph. (LGRP/NRM)

Castle Cary	1903	1913	1923	1933
Passenger tickets issued	16722	20307	20653	17012
Season tickets issued	*	*	59	79
Parcels forwarded	27531	51839	40687	45874
General goods forwarded (tons)	2126	2700	2102	1071
Coal and coke received (tons)	4189	3163	3673	1201
Other minerals received (tons)	5224	3741	3814	582
General goods received (tons)	11923	4891	3966	3827
Trucks of livestock handled	435	492	222	156

(* not available)

83. Passing under the bridge from which the previous picture was taken is a typical express from Weymouth to Paddington. No. 7909 *Heveningham Hall* is rounding the curve towards the junction on 13th August 1960. (D.Trevor Rowe)

84. The 1905 signal box was destroyed by enemy bombs on 3rd September 1942 and replaced by this 85-lever structure on 27th October of that year. No. 33001 takes the curve to the single line at 15mph on 4th June 1980, while working the diverted 09.10 Waterloo to Exeter St. Davids. (G.Gillham)

85. The goods yard had a six-ton capacity crane recorded in 1938 and closed on 3rd October 1966, but one siding was retained by the engineers. On the right of this July 1984 photograph is a backing signal with an indicator box containing stencils. The down goods loop had been lifted and a new short platform for Weymouth trains is under construction. The signal box (centre) and its mechanical signals ceased to be used on 3rd February 1985, when Westbury Panel took control of the area. ((D.H.Mitchell)

86. The down loop is seen from the same footbridge position, but on 4th October 1997 as class M7 0-4-4T no. 30053 runs round its special train from the second Yeovil Railway Festival. Up trains from Weymouth normally run into platform 2 (left) and then cross to the up line in the right background. (P.G.Barnes)

SPARKFORD

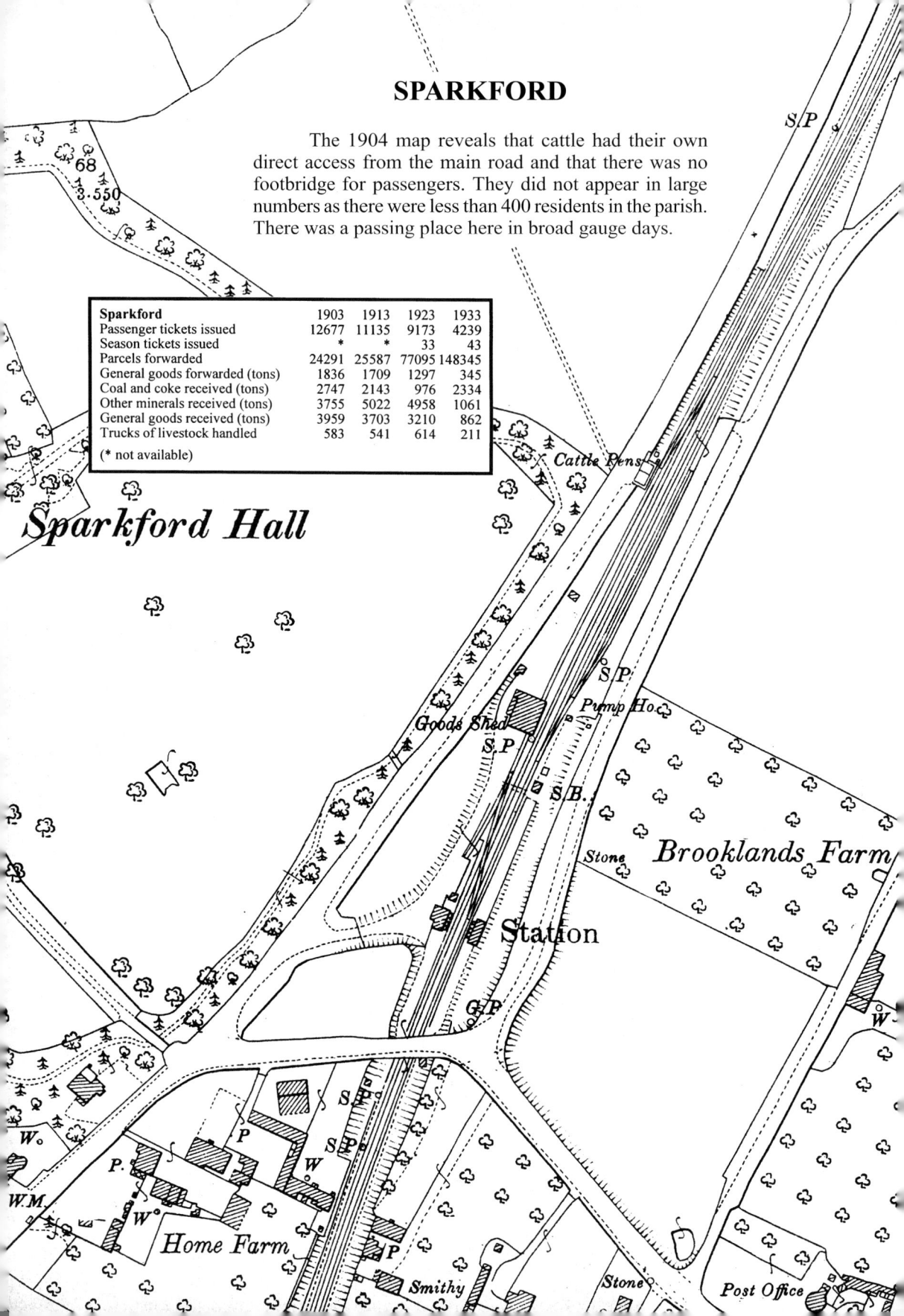

The 1904 map reveals that cattle had their own direct access from the main road and that there was no footbridge for passengers. They did not appear in large numbers as there were less than 400 residents in the parish. There was a passing place here in broad gauge days.

Sparkford	1903	1913	1923	1933
Passenger tickets issued	12677	11135	9173	4239
Season tickets issued	*	*	33	43
Parcels forwarded	24291	25587	77095	148345
General goods forwarded (tons)	1836	1709	1297	345
Coal and coke received (tons)	2747	2143	976	2334
Other minerals received (tons)	3755	5022	4958	1061
General goods received (tons)	3959	3703	3210	862
Trucks of livestock handled	583	541	614	211

(* not available)

87. An animated scene was recorded by a postcard publisher, probably around 1910, as an up train was being loaded. The structure on the left was for gentlemen - although there was no roof, ventilation grills were provided in the cast iron walls. Note the wide doorway in the goods shed for broad gauge wagons. (Lens of Sutton)

88. To record the site thoroughly, four photographs from 1st October 1966 are provided. DMUs were introduced to the route in 1959; this example is working the 14.30 from Westbury. The goods yard had closed on 7th January 1963 and the up line was removed in 1968. (C.L.Caddy)

89. Five barrows await traffic, but it had vanished to the road hauliers. Passenger traffic ceased on 3rd October 1966 officially although the last trains called on the 1st October. There were eight down and six up trains on most weekdays that year. (C.L.Caddy)

90. The map shows a pair of sidings beyond the signal box. A private siding for T.C.Raymond's sawmill was added to the refuge siding on 16th February 1929 and another was provided for the War Department on 28th May 1944, together with an additional crossover and ground frame. South of the bridge, there was a siding for a dairy trailing from the up line from 1932 to 1963, milk tankers being destined to Kensington Olympia. The realigned A303 now dominates the skyline. (C.L.Caddy)

91. The 23-lever signal box was in use from May 1877 until 30th November 1966. There had been another box four miles to the north, known as Dimmer, but its six-lever frame functioned only briefly, from 24th June 1908 to 3rd February 1909. The crossing was for the use of staff and passengers. (C.L.Caddy)

MARSTON MAGNA

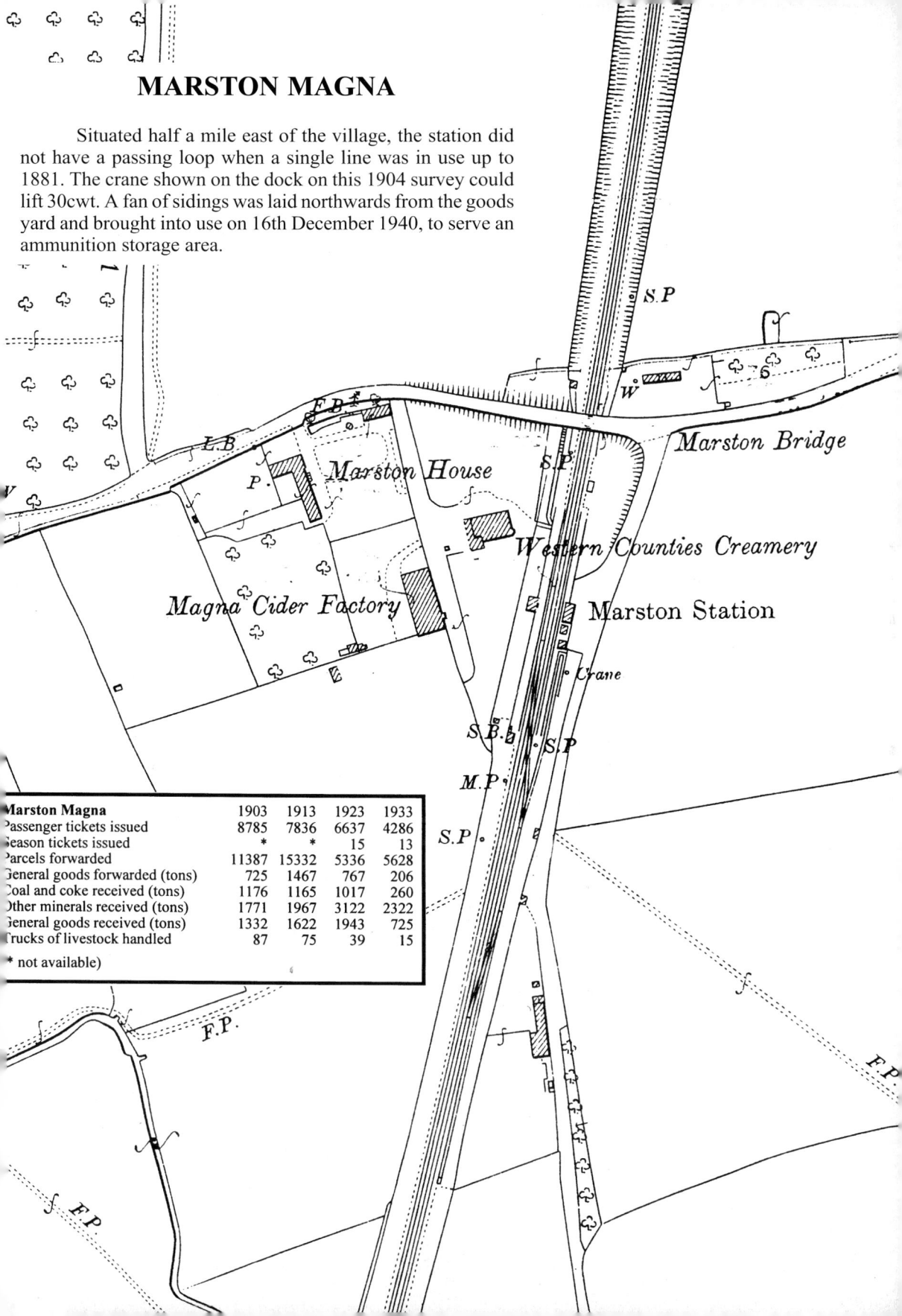

Situated half a mile east of the village, the station did not have a passing loop when a single line was in use up to 1881. The crane shown on the dock on this 1904 survey could lift 30cwt. A fan of sidings was laid northwards from the goods yard and brought into use on 16th December 1940, to serve an ammunition storage area.

Marston Magna	1903	1913	1923	1933
Passenger tickets issued	8785	7836	6637	4286
Season tickets issued	*	*	15	13
Parcels forwarded	11387	15332	5336	5628
General goods forwarded (tons)	725	1467	767	206
Coal and coke received (tons)	1176	1165	1017	260
Other minerals received (tons)	1771	1967	3122	2322
General goods received (tons)	1332	1622	1943	725
Trucks of livestock handled	87	75	39	15

(* not available)

92. A 1962 northward view includes the steps from the road to the up platform and the 1877 22-lever signal box, which was in use until 16th February 1964. Note that there was a signal arm (right) for the goods loop; the yard closed on 5th November 1962. (C.L.Caddy)

93. A panorama from the top of the steps to the up platform reveals a melancholy scene on the last day of traffic, 1st October 1966. The platforms had once been crowded with milk churns and cider barrels, but seldom passengers. The population was only 337 at the time of closure. (C.L.Caddy)

YEOVIL PEN MILL

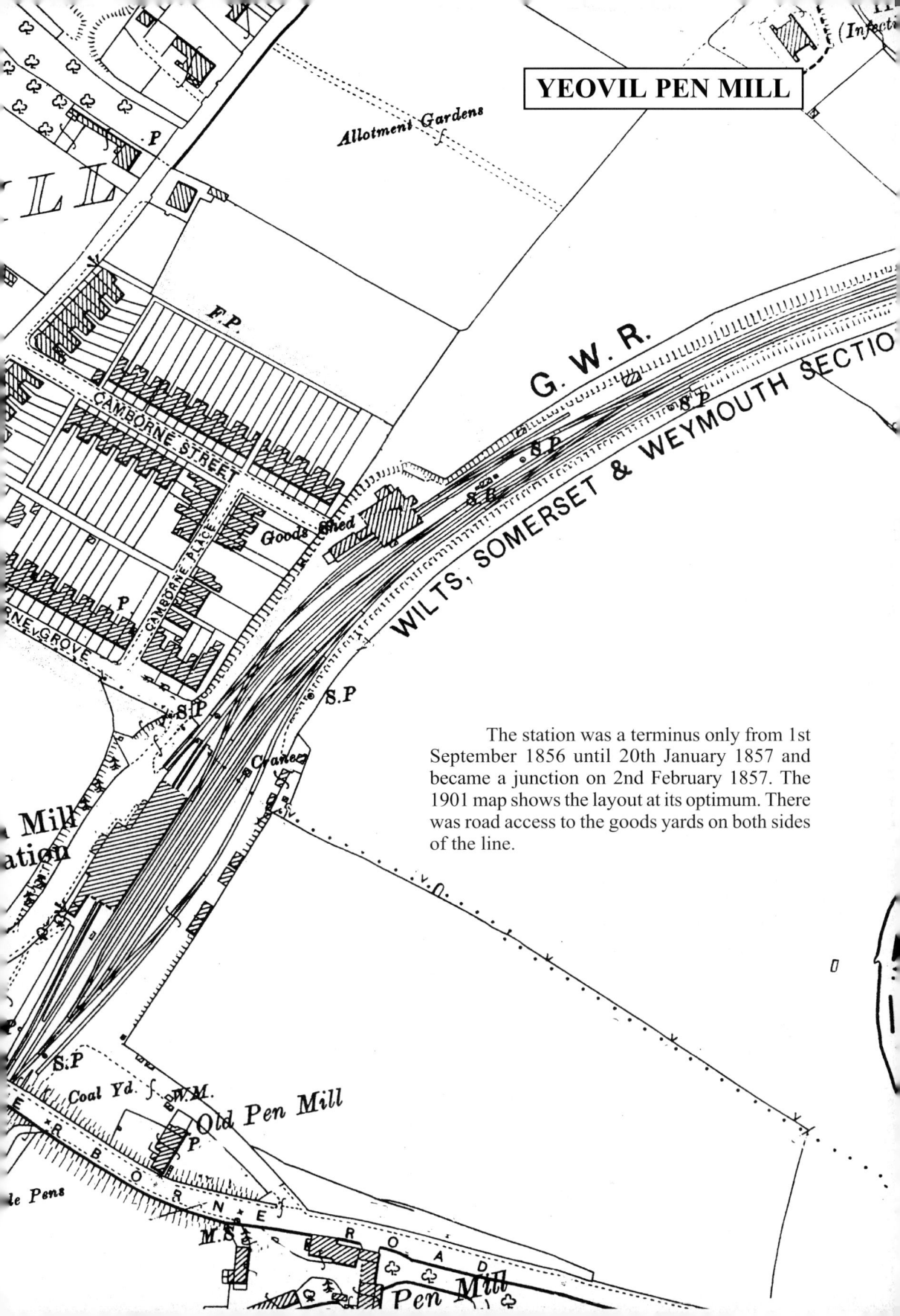

The station was a terminus only from 1st September 1856 until 20th January 1857 and became a junction on 2nd February 1857. The 1901 map shows the layout at its optimum. There was road access to the goods yards on both sides of the line.

94. A northward panorama from about 1933 features the roof over the up line and a "mobile" crane on a short length of track near a stack of round timber. The roof was removed in 1934. Some of the down sidings were used for carriage berthing. (Mowat coll.)

95. A sharper view from the same location on 10th October 1950 includes 2-6-2T no. 4543 taking water before leaving for Taunton, while an autotrain waits in the yard. The goods shed is in the left background. Channel Island boat trains ran via Bournemouth after November 1959 and there were no more direct trains to London after 1960. (D.Clayton)

96.   No. 4593 is nearly ready to start at 4.0pm for Taunton, but the driver has to oil up while the fireman waters the coal to reduce airborne dust while running bunker first on 13th June 1964. A single line tablet could be obtained from the auxiliary tablet machine (left), this being provided to save the time taken to walk from the signal box. (M.J.Messenger)

97.   August Bank Holiday in 1965 necessitated twelve coaches behind no. D7079 (right) on the 10.35 departure for Weymouth. The train had left Bristol at 08.45. No. D7015 had worked six empty coaches up from Weymouth and would return them there as the 13.15 from Yeovil Town. The goods yard closed on 12th September 1965. (R.A.Lumber)

98. Engineering work near Taunton on 30th March 1985 meant diversions via Yeovil, the rain adding to the problems. An up HST runs under Sherborne Road, having descended from Yeovil Junction. The starting signal on the right is fitted with a route indicator box. (P.G.Barnes)

99. No. 155314 is running south on 20th October 1990 as the 10.28 Bristol to Weymouth. These "Sprinter" units replaced the first generation DMUs on the route in May 1989. The signal box replaced North and South boxes on 14th February 1937 and was still controlling semaphore signals in 1999, its frame once having 65 levers. (P.G.Barnes)

100. A photograph from 9th October 1994 reveals that most of the structures had not changed in 50 years. This was the second day of the first Yeovil Railway Festival and shuttle services to the Junction were operated by two class 159 units and class M7 0-4-4T no. 30053, renumbered 30129 for the occasion. (M.Turvey)

Other views of this station and an earlier map can be found in the companion album *Yeovil to Dorchester*.

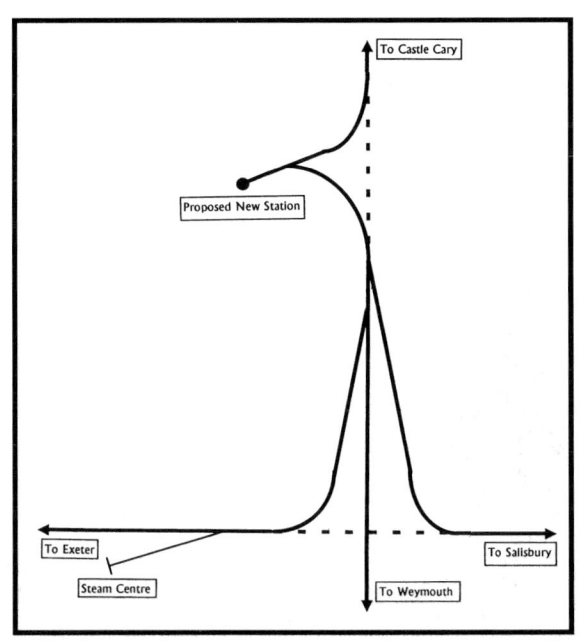

With the universal use of multiple units that can be driven from either end, it would be possible for Yeovil to have a Town station again. The former trackbeds could be used, with a fresh alignment from the 1860 curve from Salisbury to avoid reconstruction of the bridge over the Weymouth line. The lines shown dashed would not be required, but could be retained for diverted services, engineers trains, locomotive hauled extras and possible future freight traffic. If two platforms were provided, there would be opportunity for trains to pass and passenger changing would be facilitated. Land vacated at Pen Mill could provide some funds, as could local authorities concerned with the chronic road congestion in the district. An overall flat roof could be used for car parking. (Mitchell Consultancy)

SOUTH OF YEOVIL PEN MILL

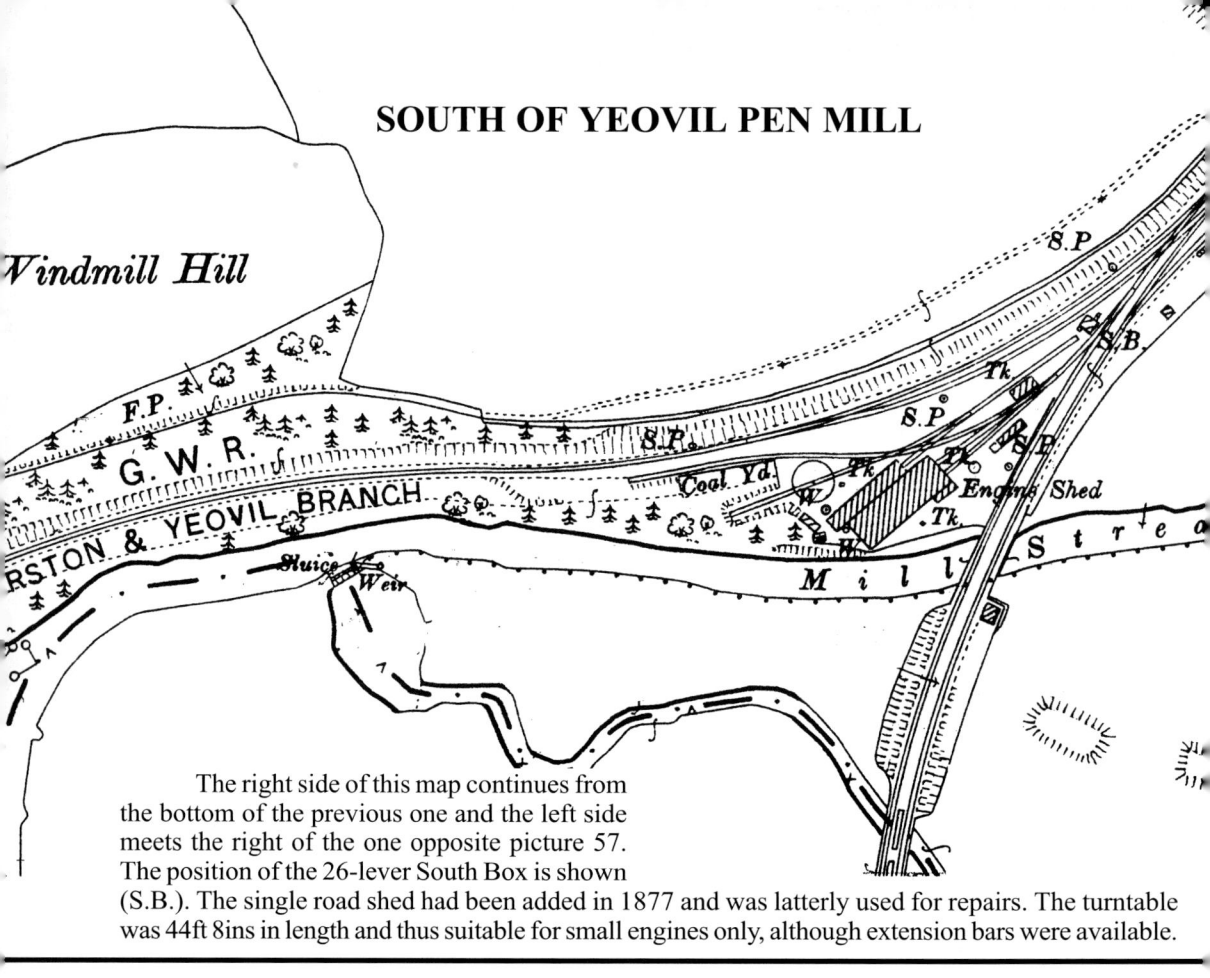

The right side of this map continues from the bottom of the previous one and the left side meets the right of the one opposite picture 57. The position of the 26-lever South Box is shown (S.B.). The single road shed had been added in 1877 and was latterly used for repairs. The turntable was 44ft 8ins in length and thus suitable for small engines only, although extension bars were available.

101. The shuttle to the Town is about to pass the ex-GWR locomotive shed on 7th July 1959. This had closed on 9th January of that year. Coach 373 had been part of a steam railmotor until 1919 and remained in use until June 1960. (H.C.Casserley)

102. The final allocation to the shed had been two class 4575 2-6-2Ts and six class 5700 0-6-0PTs. The cattle dock (left) is shown on the earliest plans and was in use until 2nd February 1964. The railbus is working the short-lived Junction-Pen Mill service on 13th October 1966 and has just passed the banner repeaters for South Junction. (H.C.Casserley)

103. Only the cattle dock and poles remain from the previous view. A diverted West of England to Paddington HST observes the 10mph speed limit on 18th May 1991, while we can observe that the points are worked by rods from the signal box at the far end of the station. (P.G.Barnes)

YEOVIL JUNCTION

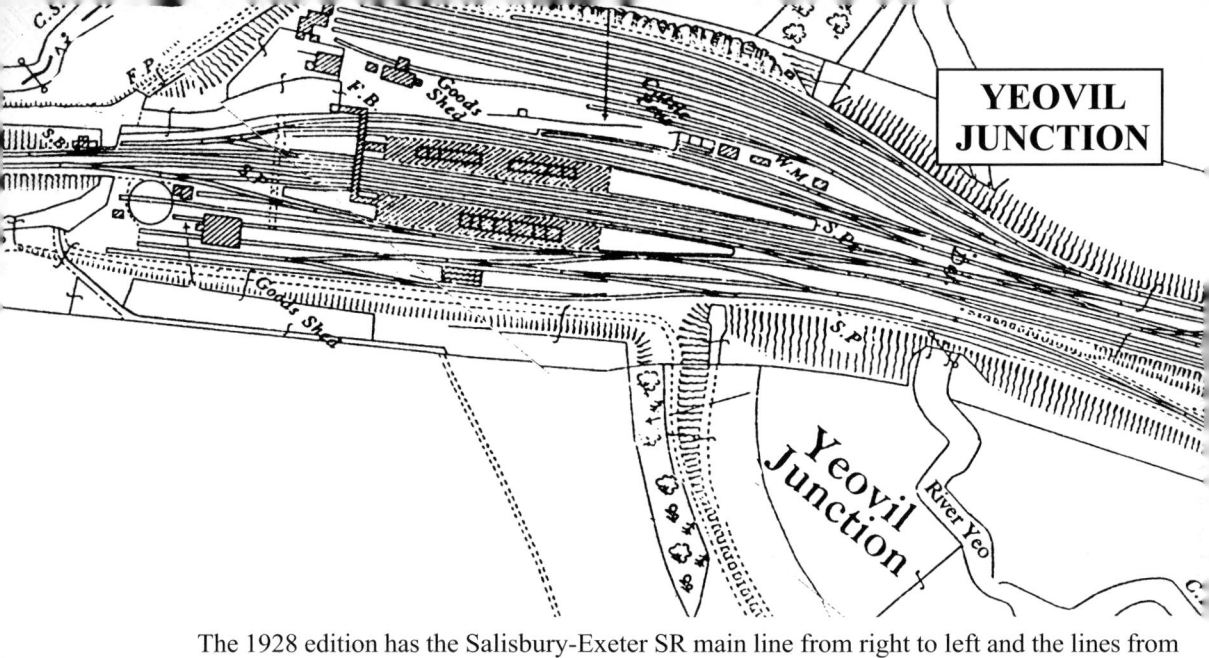

The 1928 edition has the Salisbury-Exeter SR main line from right to left and the lines from Pen Mill top right. The route to Weymouth is at the bottom; the earthwork curving away from it never carried tracks. A 1987 plan envisaged laying a track thereon and reversing Westbury-Weymouth trains at the Junction. Near the right border is evidence of the original route for LSWR trains to Yeovil. Also marked on the right page is the GWR Clifton Maybank branch, which carried freight only and was in use from 1864 to 1937 to reduce transfer traffic at Hendford. This was often about 1500 wagons per month in the 1900s.

---

104. Initially there were two island platforms separated by one track. Rearrangement in 1907-09 resulted in a separation of four tracks, as seen. In the distance is West Box, which was in use until 30th April 1967 and latterly designated "B". (Wessex coll.)

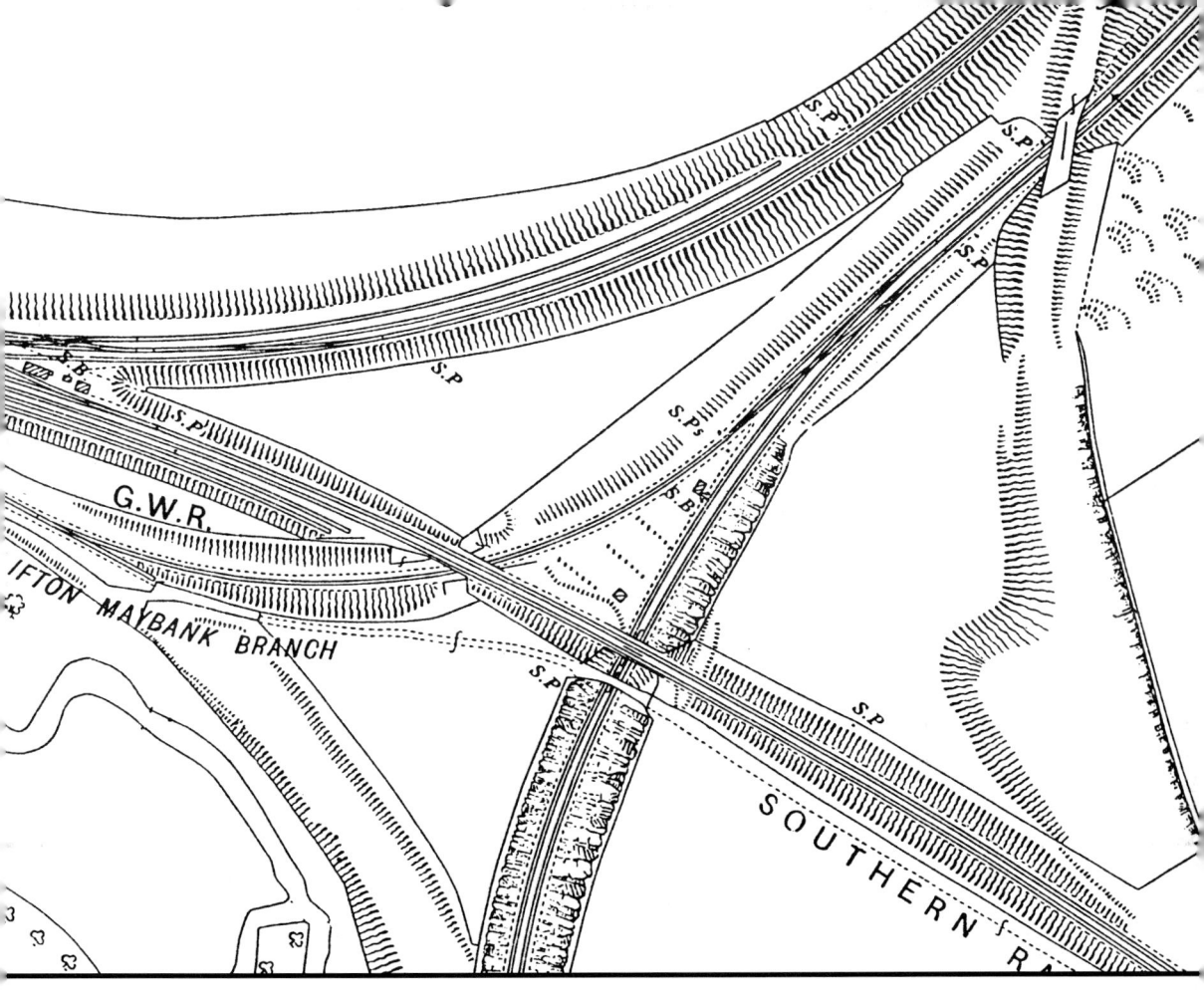

105. On the left of the previous picture is the GWR Clifton Maybank building; this is its west elevation in about 1933. It was situated on a long low island platform. The Pannier tank has arrived from Pen Mill with a transfer goods. (Mowat coll.)

106. East Box ("A") is in the centre as two coaches from Yeovil Town are propelled into platform 1. The Clifton Maybank branch curves away on the right and descends at 1 in 85. (Lens of Sutton)

107. At the end of the GWR branch was this substantial goods shed, its doorways of different sizes showing that it was intended for transfer of consignments between the gauges. However, the map opposite reveals that it had broad gauge lines only at the time of the survey. (D.Clayton)

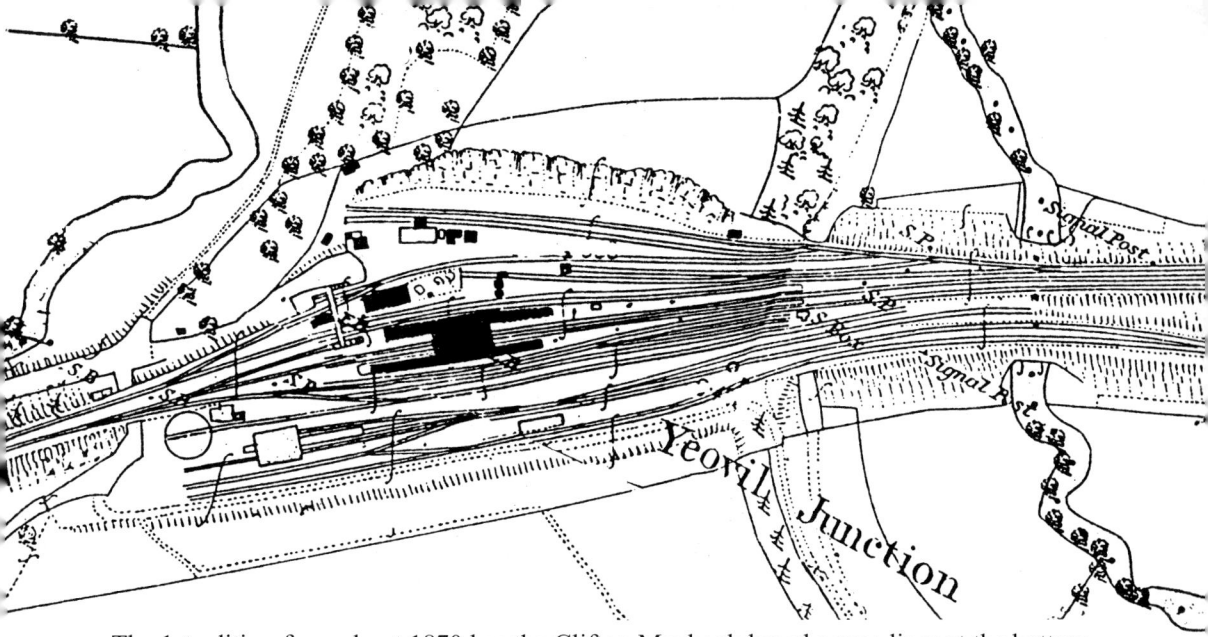

The 1st edition from about 1870 has the Clifton Maybank broad gauge lines at the bottom. The arrangement would have been suitable for passenger operation with an arrival line north of the platform, a locomotive release line west thereof and a run round loop to the south. The three passenger lines of the LSWR are also evident; the centre one was usually used by the Yeovil Town train.

108. The inefficiency of working in this area is illustrated as no. 34108 *Wincanton* arrives with the 3.50pm Yeovil Town to Waterloo service, on Sunday 9th August 1964. It will run round its lightweight train and depart at 4.0pm. The six running lines were reduced to two on 7th May 1967, these being either side of the up platform, left, but the northern one had a dead end until March 1975. (R.A.Lumber)

109. No. 33032 runs over the restored connection on 31st January 1978, the class 33 hauling most trains on the route between 1971 and 1980. Note that both lines were signalled for reversible running by that time. (T.Heavyside)

110. The powerful class 50s were employed on most trains in the 1980-93 period, this example being recorded leaving for Exeter on 3rd May 1983. Of historic interest are the disused platforms 3 and 4, the truncated footbridge that once extended to them, the ex-GWR goods shed and the 70ft vacuum operated turntable that was used by steam locomotives again from 1986, albeit only occasionally. (T.Heavyside)

111. DEMU no. 205033 nears the end of the double track section from Sherborne on 25th July 1990, as it works the 16.32 stopping service from Southampton to Yeovil Junction. On the left is the line to Pen Mill, which had been singled on 26th May 1968 and had had no regular service subsequently. (J.Scrace)

112. The Second Yeovil Railway Festival was held on 4-5th October 1997 and starred the Eastleigh Railway Preservation Society's class S15 no. 828. Behind is class 20 no. D8188 and the frame of a new engine being built by the South West Main Line Steam Company, who organised the Festivals and provide facilities for steam operators. (P.G.Barnes)

Other illustrations of this junction can be seen in our companion albums *Salisbury to Yeovil* and *Yeovil to Exeter*.

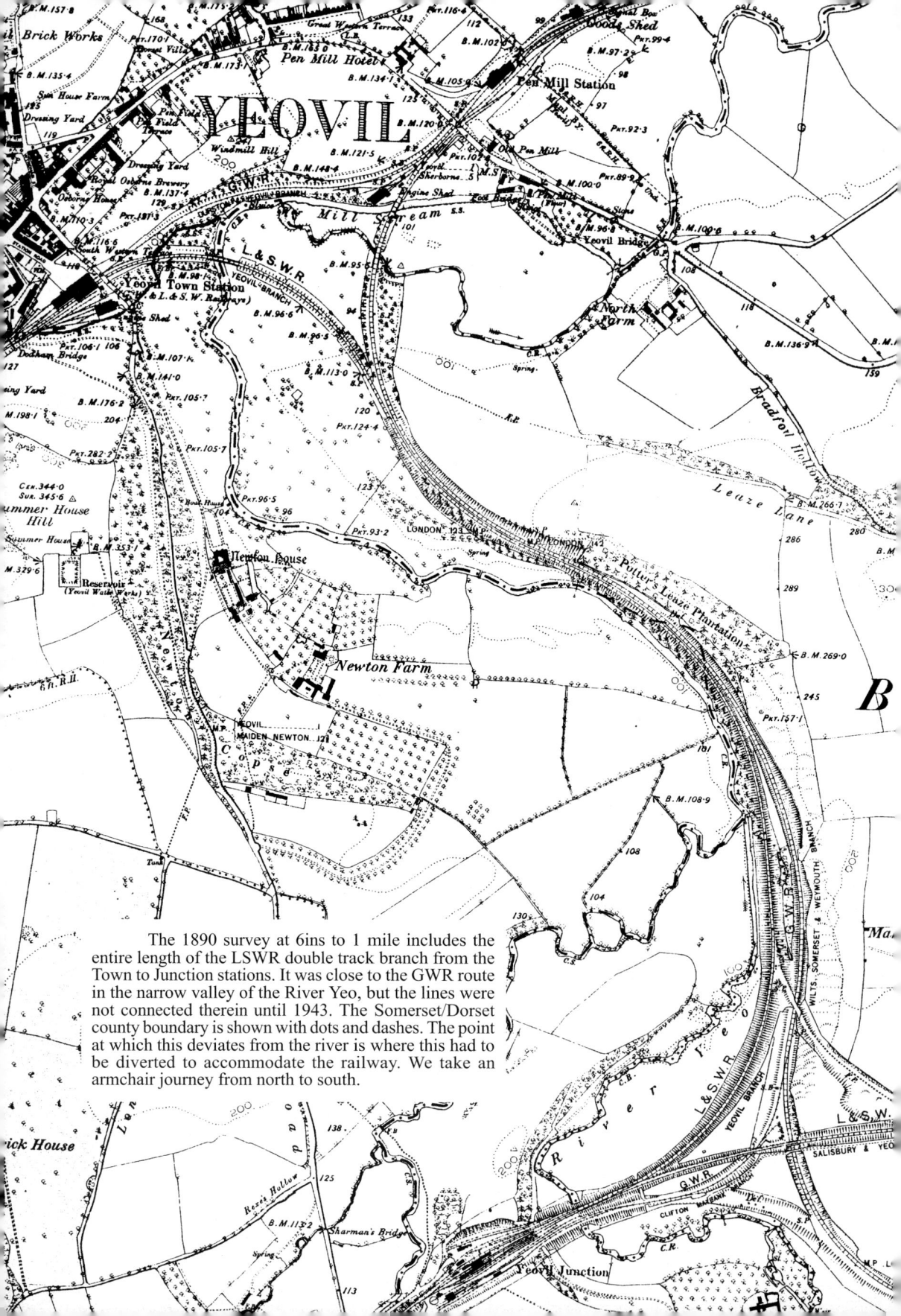

The 1890 survey at 6ins to 1 mile includes the entire length of the LSWR double track branch from the Town to Junction stations. It was close to the GWR route in the narrow valley of the River Yeo, but the lines were not connected therein until 1943. The Somerset/Dorset county boundary is shown with dots and dashes. The point at which this deviates from the river is where this had to be diverted to accommodate the railway. We take an armchair journey from north to south.

4. Around Yeovil

113. We look east from Newton Road bridge at Yeovil Town on 26th October 1963 as the 2.51pm from the Junction approaches the station behind one of the 4800 class 0-4-2Ts. The line to Pen Mill is on the left. (E.Wilmshurst)

114. The twilight of the branch is portrayed well in this dramatic view of an AC railbus running towards the Junction on 27th February 1965. These two-axle vehicles were first used at Yeovil on 28th December 1964. The former GWR main line is on the left. (M.J.Messenger)

115. The point of convergence of the two routes was photographed on 30th March 1985, the trackbed of the Yeovil Town line being on the right. A DMU from Weymouth waits at the junction that was created in 1968 following the singling of the lines. No. 50005 takes a diverted train towards the Junction. (P.G.Barnes)

116. The Canadian Army helped to lay connections between the GWR and SR routes for emergency wartime use. They are seen from the south on 3rd August 1958, as the 9.30am Exeter Central to Weymouth passes, hauled by ex-GWR 2-6-2T no. 4133. The 33-lever box was opened specially to allow the train to run north, over the crossover, earlier that day. The connection was used regularly between 3rd October 1966 and 5th May 1968, but the Yeovil Town lines closed on 1st March 1967. (R.A.Lumber)

GREAT WESTERN RAILWAY.

DAILY EXCURSIONS TO WEYMOUTH

EXCURSION TICKETS TO WEYMOUTH

Are now issued DAILY (SUNDAYS included) as under:—

STATIONS.	On Week-days. a.m.	On Sundays. a.m.	1st Cl. s. d.	Cov. Cars. s. d.
Bristol	6 40	8 0	10 0	5 0
Bath	7 5	8 30	8 0	4 0
Bradford	7 32	8 55	7 0	3 6
Trowbridge	7 45	9 10	7 0	3 6
Westbury	8 10	9 20	7 0	3 6
Frome	8 24	9 35	7 0	3 6
Chippenham	7 25	—	8 0	4 0
Melksham	7 40	—	8 0	4 0
Witham	8 36	9 47	6 0	3 0
Bruton	8 50	10 0	6 0	3 0
Castle Carey	9 0	10 8	6 0	3 0
Sparkford	9 10	10 18	6 0	3 0
Yeovil	9 30	10 35	5 0	2 6

On Week-days the Tickets will be available for Return by the Train leaving Weymouth at 6.30 p.m., and on Sundays at 5.0 p.m.

NO LUGGAGE ALLOWED.

The Tickets are not transferable, and are available on the day of issue only, and only to and from the Stations named upon them, and by the Trains specified above; if used otherwise, the full Ordinary Fares will be charged.

July 14th, 1870.   J. GRIERSON, *General Manager.*

McCorquodale & Co., Printers, "The Armoury," Southwark.

117. Yeovil Junction is in the distance as a DMU runs round the curve on its way to Pen Mill on 13th April 1968. On the left is a train from Waterloo, while in the foreground are the abutments of the bridge that carried trains between Salisbury and Yeovil Town between 1860 and 1870. The span was in place until 1937. (R.A.Lumber)

118. Near the left border of the picture above was Clifton Maybank junction. It is seen here from the south in 1925, as a train proceeds towards Weymouth. The first box was in use from 1877 to 1896; this one served until 7th June 1937 and had 21 levers. (Unknown)

119. Looking across the Salisbury lines on Easter Monday 11th April 1966, we watch class 35 no. D7093 accelerating towards Weymouth, the rear coach being near the site of the 1860 bridge. Half way along the train is the site of Clifton Maybank junction. (R.A.Lumber)

120. Part of the Clifton Maybank branch was relaid as the Yeovil Country Railway and 1921 Peckett 0-4-0 ST *Pectin* operated brake van trips during the 1997 Yeovil Railway Festival. Once again Yeovil has become a source of pleasure for admirers of steam, with regular visits of railtours. (P.G.Barnes)

MP Middleton Press

Easebourne Lane, Midhurst, West Sussex. GU29 9AZ Tel: 01730 813169 Fax: 01730 812601
If books are not available from your local transport stockist, order direct with cheque, Visa or Mastercard, post free UK.

BRANCH LINES
Branch Line to Allhallows
Branch Lines around Ascot
Branch Line to Ashburton
Branch Lines around Bodmin
Branch Line to Bude
Branch Lines around Canterbury
Branch Lines around Chard & Yeovil
Branch Line to Cheddar
Branch Lines around Cromer
Branch Lines to East Grinstead
Branch Lines to Effingham Junction
Branch Lines around Exmouth
Branch Line to Fairford
Branch Line to Hawkhurst
Branch Line to Hayling
Branch Lines to Horsham
Branch Line to Ilfracombe
Branch Line to Kingswear
Branch Lines to Launceston & Princetown
Branch Lines to Longmoor
Branch Line to Looe
Branch Line to Lyme Regis
Branch Lines around March
Branch Lines around Midhurst
Branch Line to Minehead
Branch Line to Moretonhampstead
Branch Lines to Newport (IOW)
Branch Line to Padstow
Branch Lines around Plymouth
Branch Line to Selsey
Branch Lines around Sheerness
Branch Line to Tenterden
Branch Lines to Torrington
Branch Lines to Tunbridge Wells
Branch Line to Upwell
Branch Lines around Weymouth
Branch Lines around Wimborne
Branch Lines around Wisbech

NARROW GAUGE BRANCH LINES
Branch Line to Lynton
Branch Lines around Portmadoc 1923-46
Branch Lines around Porthmadog 1954-94
Two-Foot Gauge Survivors

SOUTH COAST RAILWAYS
Ashford to Dover
Brighton to Eastbourne
Chichester to Portsmouth
Dover to Ramsgate
Hastings to Ashford
Portsmouth to Southampton
Southampton to Bournemouth
Worthing to Chichester

SOUTHERN MAIN LINES
Bromley South to Rochester
Charing Cross to Orpington
Crawley to Littlehampton
Dartford to Sittingbourne
East Croydon to Three Bridges
Epsom to Horsham
Exeter to Barnstaple
Exeter to Tavistock
Faversham to Dover
Haywards Heath to Seaford
London Bridge to East Croydon
Orpington to Tonbridge
Salisbury to Yeovil
Swanley to Ashford
Tavistock to Plymouth
Victoria to East Croydon
Waterloo to Windsor
Waterloo to Woking
Woking to Portsmouth
Woking to Southampton
Yeovil to Exeter

EASTERN MAIN LINES
Fenchurch Street to Barking

COUNTRY RAILWAY ROUTES
Andover to Southampton
Bournemouth to Evercreech Jn.
Burnham to Evercreech Junction
Croydon to East Grinstead
Didcot to Winchester
Fareham to Salisbury
Frome to Bristol
Guildford to Redhill
Porthmadog to Blaenau
Reading to Basingstoke
Reading to Guildford
Redhill to Ashford
Salisbury to Westbury
Stratford Upon Avon to Cheltenham
Strood to Paddock Wood
Taunton to Barnstaple
Wenford Bridge to Fowey
Westbury to Bath
Woking to Alton
Yeovil to Dorchester

GREAT RAILWAY ERAS
Ashford from Steam to Eurostar
Clapham Junction 50 years of change
Festiniog in the Fifties
Festiniog in the Sixties
Isle of Wight Lines 50 years of change
Railways to Victory 1944-46

LONDON SUBURBAN RAILWAYS
Caterham and Tattenham Corner
Charing Cross to Dartford
Clapham Jn. to Beckenham Jn.
Crystal Palace and Catford Loop
East London Line
Finsbury Park to Alexandra Palace
Holborn Viaduct to Lewisham
Kingston and Hounslow Loops
Lewisham to Dartford
Lines around Wimbledon
London Bridge to Addiscombe
North London Line
South London Line
West Croydon to Epsom
West London Line
Willesden Junction to Richmond
Wimbledon to Epsom

STEAMING THROUGH
Steaming through Cornwall
Steaming through the Isle of Wight
Steaming through Kent
Steaming through West Hants
Steaming through West Sussex

TRAMWAY CLASSICS
Aldgate & Stepney Tramways
Barnet & Finchley Tramways
Bath Tramways
Bournemouth & Poole Tramways
Brighton's Tramways
Camberwell & W.Norwood Tramways
Clapham & Streatham Tramways
Dover's Tramways
East Ham & West Ham Tramways
Edgware and Willesden Tramways
Eltham & Woolwich Tramways
Embankment & Waterloo Tramways
Enfield & Wood Green Tramways
Exeter & Taunton Tramways
Gosport & Horndean Tramways
Greenwich & Dartford Tramways
Hampstead & Highgate Tramways
Hastings Tramways
Holborn & Finsbury Tramways
Ilford & Barking Tramways
Kingston & Wimbledon Tramways
Lewisham & Catford Tramways
Liverpool Tramways 1. Eastern Routes
Liverpool Tramways 2. Southern Routes
Maidstone & Chatham Tramways
North Kent Tramways
Portsmouth's Tramways
Reading Tramways
Seaton & Eastbourne Tramways
Shepherds Bush & Uxbridge Tramways
Southampton Tramways
Southend-on-sea Tramways
Southwark & Deptford Tramways
Stamford Hill Tramways
Thanet's Tramways
Victoria & Lambeth Tramways
Waltham Cross & Edmonton Tramways
Walthamstow & Leyton Tramways
Wandsworth & Battersea Tramways

TROLLEYBUS CLASSICS
Croydon Trolleybuses
Bournemouth Trolleybuses
Hastings Trolleybuses
Maidstone Trolleybuses
Reading Trolleybuses
Woolwich & Dartford Trolleybuses

WATERWAY ALBUMS
Kent and East Sussex Waterways
London to Portsmouth Waterway
Surrey Waterways
West Sussex Waterways

MILITARY BOOKS and VIDEO
Battle over Portsmouth
Battle over Sussex 1940
Blitz over Sussex 1941-42
Bombers over Sussex 1943-45
Bognor at War
Military Defence of West Sussex
Secret Sussex Resistance
Sussex Home Guard
War on the Line
War on the Line VIDEO

OTHER BOOKS and VIDEO
Betwixt Petersfield & Midhurst
Changing Midhurst
Garraway Father & Son
Index to all Stations
South Eastern & Chatham Railways
London Chatham & Dover Railway